KW-221-916

STRATFORD PAPERS

1968–69

Shakespeare in the New World

edited by B. A. W. Jackson

McMaster University Library Press

Irish University Press

© McMaster University Library Press,
Canada, 1972

This edition is distributed in India exclusively by the

Lyall Book Depot
Chaura Bazaar
Ludhiana (P.B.–India)

ISBN 0 7165 0002 7 (IUP)

ISBN 0-9690270-1-X (McMaster)

All forms of micropublishing
© *Irish University Microforms   Shannon   Ireland*

Irish University Press   Shannon   Ireland

FILMSET AND PRINTED IN THE REPUBLIC OF IRELAND AT SHANNON
BY ROBERT HOGG PRINTER TO IRISH UNIVERSITY PRESS

KING ALFRED'S COLLEGE
WINCHESTER

822.33
JAC

13067

STRATFORD PAPERS
1968–69

ACKNOWLEDGEMENTS

For permission to reproduce material in this collection of papers, acknowledgement is made to the following:

'Imaginary Forces and the Ways of Comedy'—

The Society of Authors on behalf of the Bernard Shaw Estate for the extract from *Saint Joan* by Bernard Shaw.

J. M. Dent and Sons Ltd, and the Trustees of the Joseph Conrad Estate for the extract from *Heart of Darkness* by Joseph Conrad.

Granada Publishing, and Harcourt Brace Jovanovich, Inc., for the extract from E. E. Cummings' poem (*Complete Works 1913–35*, published by MacGibbon and Kee, and *Poems 1923–1954*, published by Harcourt Brace Jovanovich).

Material contained in the paper by Anthony Burgess was first published by Jonathan Cape Ltd and Random House/Knopf Inc. as part of Chapter 15 ('Royal Deaths') from *Shakespeare* by Anthony Burgess, © Anthony Burgess 1970. It is reproduced here under licence from the publishers.

CONTENTS

Preface vii

Imaginary Forces and the Ways of Comedy
J. PERCY SMITH I

Measure for Measure: A Comedy GEOFFREY DURRANT . 21

Ben Jonson and Alchemy ROBERTSON DAVIES . . 40

Shakespeare in West Africa MARTIN BANHAM . . 61

Notes on Acting Mercutio LEO CICERI . . . 70

Hamlet: World Première ANTHONY BURGESS . . 75

Shakespeare and Dance ALAN BRISSENDEN . . . 85

Measure for Measure J. A. LAVIN 97

The Langham Regime HERBERT WHITTAKER . . 114

'My crown, mine own ambition and my Queen' (on
playing Claudius) LEO CICERI 124

Shakespeare in the New World MURRAY D. EDWARDS . 137

The Still and the Smile W. B. READY . . . 151

PREFACE

This volume contains a selection of the papers delivered at the 1968 and 1969 sessions of the Shakespeare Seminars. Our publications are now up to date, with single volumes of *The Stratford Papers* for each of the first five years of the seminars (1960–64), a volume including papers from the years 1965–67 and this present book. The first decade thus represented, we plan to begin the second with a single volume for 1970 containing the papers delivered that summer.

The purpose of these publications is to offer to our readers a selection of the talks given during the meetings of the seminars on Shakespeare sponsored at Stratford, Ontario, each summer by McMaster University in co-operation with the Festival Theatre. The original audiences for these lectures were made up of about 150 persons drawn to the seminars by their common interest in Shakespeare and in the theatre. By publishing these items, very much as they were first delivered at Stratford, we hope to make them available to a larger audience of the same kind. Since the original audiences were a cross-section of theatre-goers, from scholars and other specialists in Shakespeare to enthusiastic amateurs of the world of theatre, it is our belief that a similar cross-section of readers will enjoy this book.

The Shakespeare Seminars are for people who find it agreeable to spend at least a part of their holidays in going to the theatre and in engaging in a week's dialogue, both formal and informal, about it. Since the Festival Theatre has a special concern with Shakespeare, the emphasis in this volume is on his works, and, of course, what is contained here represents the more formal part of the proceedings, but the seminars are also concerned with the theatre in general and with drama other than Shakespeare's, and much of the seminar programme is provided by activities and entertainments that do not lend themselves to inclusion in a record such as this: the theatre performances, panel discussions with actors and critics, formal discussion sessions for small groups and, perhaps best of all, the continuing informal discussion among the members at bar and table and elsewhere.

While these ephemera cannot be recorded, we can record our

gratitude to all those who participated in them. Many of these were the hard-working people of the Festival Theatre itself. Where much more is due, we can give only our thanks to Jane Casson, Dolores Sutton, Maureen O'Brien, Mervyn Blake, Donald Davis, Salem Ludwig, Barry MacGregor, William Needles, Powys Thomas and Kenneth Welsh among others. These people provided many of the sprightlier moments of the seminars but, even more important, they contributed largely to the sense the members had of being in touch with the theatre itself, the centre of the summer festival.

Since I last wrote a preface to one of these volumes, the seminars have lost two friends and benefactors. John Crow, late of King's College, London, died in October 1969, and Leo Ciceri of the Festival Company was killed in an automobile accident in August 1970. Mr Crow contributed to the seminars as a speaker and discussion leader during eight of their eleven summers. His learning was formidable, his wit legendary and his kindness enormous. He had seen as much theatre as any man in his time, and his admiration of the festival productions was uncompromising. Above all, he was, in an age when individualism is much admired and rarely found, a genuine individual with an unquenchable gaiety of spirit, an impeccable eye for the ridiculous and the absurd and a Johnsonian gift of expression. There can be no substitute for the irreplaceable John Crow.

Two of Leo Ciceri's pieces appear in this book. They are short, for each served simply as an introduction to a ninety-minute session in which he fielded questions from his audience. Those who were so fortunate as to be at those meetings will recall Mr Ciceri's contributions to the seminars; others will remember his part in formal discussion groups, his intelligence and charm, above all his captivating vitality. His work with the seminars constituted a very small proportion of Leo Ciceri's enormous contribution to the festival seasons, but it was something that was typical of him, reflecting as it did his deep concern for the theatre and his generosity in serving its interests. Among the many who regret his death and recall with gratitude the pleasure he gave them summer after summer, the members of the seminar have a special reason for recording their thanks and their sense of loss.

McMaster University   B. A. W. Jackson

IMAGINARY FORCES AND THE
WAYS OF COMEDY
J. Percy Smith

It is one of the common observations of criticism that Shakespeare's art, like Homer's, does not identify the poet's personality. We admonish ourselves repeatedly—and rightly—to bear in mind that when Hamlet, Richard or Feste speaks, it is not Shakespeare who speaks: it is Hamlet, Richard or Feste, in a play that contains also Claudius, Bolingbroke or Malvolio, and that each of them is Shakespeare's creation. When we find a preference for certain characters or speeches or points of view, the preference is ours, not Shakespeare's. Even when we take the larger view and look at the plays as artistic wholes, it is dangerous to assume that our perceptions reveal more of Shakespeare than they do of ourselves. If indeed the plays become for us the comments on a life of allegory, we need to ask whether the allegory is Shakespeare's or John Keats's or our own. No doubt it is tempting to see much of Shakespeare in Prospero, that worker of magic who, deeply reconciled to humanity, decides to drown his book and retire to Milan to spend a third of his time thinking about his grave. Was not Shakespeare when he wrote *The Tempest* about to retire from the magic of the theatre to the quietness of Stratford? The theory has a certain charm; but one may wonder how well it chimes with the story that the blessed Heaven-sent Bringer of Light (as Carlyle was to call him) died after a drinking bout.

Having thus dutifully reminded myself of the dangers of the personal heresy in Shakespearian criticism, I shall doubtless now proceed to do as some ungracious pastors do, myself the primrose path of dalliance tread, and reck not my own rede.

I should say at the beginning that I do not intend to review, much less join in speculation about, the various theories concerning the occasion for which *A Midsummer Night's Dream* was written. The question has its historical interest, of course. I confess, however, that I cannot feel greatly concerned whether Shakespeare wrote the play for a wedding and subsequently adapted it to the public theatre, as many scholars claim; whether he wrote it for the theatre and subsequently adapted it for a wedding, as has also been argued; whether the wedding was that of Lord A and the countess of B, or Sir XY and Mistress Z, or some threefold combination of such happy occasions, as Professor Dover Wilson is now inclined to think. The significant fact for us, surely, is that this play has continued to interest and delight audiences and has inspired artists and musicians (Blake, Hogarth, Purcell, Mendelssohn, Benjamin Britten, for example) through the centuries since it was written. (It seems to have had a somewhat thin time in the Restoration period, but too much attention has been paid to Samuel Pepys's adverse comment. After all, he was only an administrator.) When a work of art exhibits such vitality, it must surely be because it speaks to and for forces in our natures—and perhaps in life itself—that are deep and abiding. This is not to suggest that all ages, much less all individuals, will perceive or describe those forces in the same ways or share identical responses. It does, I think, mean that one of the most rewarding things that we can do in contemplating such a work—whether a play, a picture or a piece of music—is to try to identify and understand our responses and to share them with others. By these means they may themselves be both deepened and clarified. What follows is of course nothing more than the comment of one individual, living in a particular time and place.

It seems to me that there is one subject on which Shakespeare's thought may with some confidence be traced. That subject is his own art—or arts, if you prefer—of poetry and the theatre. In the sonnets and plays there is a good deal of comment on these, on the special qualities of mind that pertain to them, on the dangers and difficulties that they present to the artist, on the relation of them to the beholder, whether reader or audience. It is possible that a systematic study might reveal a line of development in Shakespeare's presentation of these matters and some alteration of his attitude. It would be surprising if that were not so. Even a rather cursory consideration leads one to note a series of reflections that are sober and self-consistent. The fact that they are assigned to various characters in the plays seems not to disturb their general tenor. I should like here to examine one or two of these as they bear on *A Midsummer Night's Dream,* having in mind that sometimes an Elizabethan primrose path may help us to get through a modern brier-patch.

In *A Midsummer Night's Dream,* for the first time in the plays, Shakespeare gives certain of his characters something to say directly about poetry and about the theatre. The two passages in which he does so occur in the same scene and involve the same individuals. At the beginning of Act V, the lovers have told the story of their night in the woods—a night that, as we of the audience are aware, had even more fantastic things in it than the lovers knew. Hippolyta comments on the strange story that the lovers have told, and Theseus replies with a much-quoted speech:

> More strange than true: I never may believe
> These antique fables, nor these fairy toys.
> Lovers and madmen have such seething brains,
> Such shaping fantasies, that apprehend
> More than cool reason ever comprehends.
> The lunatic, the lover, and the poet,
> Are of imagination all compact:
> One sees more devils than vast hell can hold,
> That is the madman; the lover, all as frantic,
> Sees Helen's beauty in a brow of Egypt.
> The poet's eye, in a fine frenzy rolling,
> Doth glance from heaven to earth, from earth to heaven,
> And, as the imagination bodies forth
> The forms of things unknown, the poet's pen
> Turns them to shapes, and gives to airy nothing
> A local habitation and a name.
> Such tricks hath strong imagination
> That, if it would but apprehend some joy,
> It comprehends some bringer of that joy,
> Or in the night, imagining some fear,
> How easy is a bush supposed a bear!

'More strange than true. I never may believe/These antique fables, nor these fairy toys.' Theseus does not actually say that the lovers have been telling lies, though he comes little short of doing so. He does speak with the voice of the rationalist, for whom what happens ought to have some sensible and understandable explanation. For him reason is cool, comprehending, stable—as against those tricks that are the products of the seething brains and strong imaginations of lunatics, lovers and poets.

We need not be surprised at Theseus. Without attempting to examine here Renaissance ideas about the nature and worth of the imagination—or fantasy, as it was alternatively called—we may note that he is expressing a common attitude. In general it may be said that imagination was considered to be that part of the mind opposed to—or the counterpart of—reason. Given the common Renaissance view that reason was the noblest quality of

3

man—godlike reason, Hamlet calls it—it is not surprising that the imagination should be regarded with a good deal of suspicion, nor that the necessity of keeping it under the restraints of reason should be urged. For reason takes its stand on fact, on what can be known and understood: to use Theseus's word, it 'comprehends'. Imagination, however, apprehends: it reaches beyond what is known; it makes pictures of the unknown, the unreal, the mysterious. Moreover, it not only makes pictures, but through them it stirs our feelings and organizes our attitudes and our purposes, sometimes in ways that the reason may find unacceptable. Robert Burton gives us a literary anatomist's account of it:

> Phantasy, or imagination . . . is an inner sense which doth more fully examine the species perceived by *common sense,* of things present or absent, and keeps them longer, recalling them to mind again, or making new of his own. In time of sleep this faculty is free, and many times conceives strange, stupend, absurd shapes, as in sick men we commonly observe. His *organ* is the middle cell of the brain: his objects all the species communicated to him by the *common sense,* by the comparison of which he feigns infinite others unto himself. In *melancholy* men this faculty is most powerful and strong, and often hurts, producing many monstrous and prodigious things, especially if it be stirred up by some terrible object presented to it from *common sense* or *memory*. In Poets and Painters imagination forcibly works, as appears by their several fictions, anticks, images . . . In men it is subject and governed by reason, or at least should be; but in brutes it hath no superior and is *ratio brutorum,* all the reason they have.

Shakespeare would hardly have accepted Burton's implied judgement that poets and painters are not men. He was, however, well aware of the dangerous power of imagination and of the view that Burton was to present. Macbeth begins his tragic course with horrible imaginings and a murder that is but fantastical. Hamlet is first offended because his mother's behaviour has been that of a beast that wants discourse of reason, and much of the action (or inaction, if you prefer) of the play results from his inability to determine whether or not his imaginations are as foul as Vulcan's stithy.

Two points: Professor Dover Wilson has argued, on the basis of strong textual evidence, that when Shakespeare first wrote Theseus's speech, he made no reference to the poet. If Wilson is right, then Shakespeare originally would have had Theseus

4

presenting the imagination only as the deceptive force that operated fearfully in the minds of madmen; more engagingly, if not more trustworthily, in those of lovers. It needed the cool check of reason. I cannot accept Wilson's view that Shakespeare added the lines about the poet simply as a joke at the expense of his own craft. I take it that the addition of the poet to the list of those in whom imagination works freely not only extends the list, but gives the imagination a new function, making it positively creative. Theseus's speech, so amended, foreshadows both the fear that the rationalist eighteenth century was to have of the imagination, and also the recognition, by such people as Samuel Johnson, of its value to artistic creation. In later years, Coleridge attempted to deal with the imagination by refining definition and determining precisely what was the nature of the imaginative force that operated in the mind of a poet. Shakespeare, however, had not been much interested in the process of philosophical analysis, nor were the artists who came after Coleridge. Dickens's comments on Mr Gradgrind are echoed in the cry of Peter Cauchon in the epilogue to Shaw's *Saint Joan:*

> Must then a Christ perish in torment in every age to save those that have no imagination?

The second point has to do with Hippolyta's rejoinder to Theseus's speech. She is almost turning the tables on her rationalist bridegroom as she points out that, however readily he may dismiss the story that the lovers have told, the obvious fact is that something wonderful—indeed, transfiguring—has taken place. The implicit challenge to him to offer an explanation is—fortunately for him, we may think—interrupted by the entry of the four young people.

At all events, it is clear enough that Shakespeare had come to recognize the value—not to say necessity—of imagination to his art. Perhaps his addition to the passage resulted from his reading Sir Philip Sidney; for what Theseus says about the skill of the poet's pen is not very different from what Sidney had said in his *Apology for Poetry:*

> Onely the Poet, disdayning to be tied to any such subjection, lifted up with the vigor of his owne invention, doth growe in effect another nature, in making things either better then Nature bringeth forth, or, quite newe, formes such as never were in Nature.

But it is not only the poet's art for which the imagination is necessary: the art of the theatre requires it. Nor is it enough that the playwright and the actors should exercise it. Shortly after Theseus's speech to which I have referred, the 'tedious brief scene' of Pyramus and Thisbe is brought in. After Wall has discharged his part, Hippolyta turns to Theseus and says,

> This is the silliest stuff that e'er I heard,

to which Theseus responds,

> The best in this kind are but shadows: and the worst are no worse, if imagination amend them;

and Hippolyta rejoins,

> It must be your imagination then, and not theirs.

Unless I am mistaken, this is the first occasion on which Shakespeare introduced into a play comment on the art of the theatre; it is the more notable therefore that the comment should have to do with the role of imagination. Bottom and his fellows had their forerunners in Armado and the other Worthies of *Love's Labour's Lost;* those too came in for drubbing comments from their courtly audience. Theseus's remark, however, extends not merely to the amateurs of *Pyramus and Thisbe,* but to every actor, including those professionals of whom Shakespeare was one: even the best of them are but shadows.

We may find that the word 'shadows', so frequently used by Shakespeare, carries with it suggestive overtones of Plato's cave. We should remind ourselves that as Shakespeare uses it, it means 'reflections', as in a looking glass. So the realist Bolingbroke, newly crowned, tells the deposed Richard, who dashes to the ground the mirror in which he has been studying himself,

> The shadow of your sorrow hath destroyed
> The shadow of your face.

And Hamlet, in the midst of giving a practical lecture to the actors, pauses to remind them that the function of their art is to hold a mirror up to nature. To distort the reflection is to condemn the art; for at best they are, as he has already said, abstract and brief chronicles.

To his implicit reminder to his colleagues, through Theseus, of the evanescence of their art, Shakespeare adds, through Hippolyta, an admonition to the audience: in this work of creation you must collaborate, and the basis of the collaboration is the imagination. The exchange is a brief one, but it looks forward to the great prologue of *Henry V:*

6

O for a Muse of fire, that would ascend
The brightest heaven of invention!

. . . . Can this cockpit hold
The vasty fields of France? Or may we cram
Within this wooden O the very casques
That did affright the air at Agincourt?
O, pardon: since a crooked figure may
Attest in place a million;
And let us, ciphers to this great accompt,
On your imaginary forces work: . . .

Piece out our imperfections with your thoughts.
Into a thousand parts divide one man,
And make imaginary puissance.
Think when we talk of horses, that you see them,
Printing their proud hooves i' th' receiving earth.
For 'tis your thoughts that now must deck our kings,
Carry them here and there; jumping o'er times;
Turning th' accomplishment of many years
Into an hour-glass.

The intention could not be clearer. A play can have its full being
only when actors and audience join together in an experience that
at its best is mutual and magical, transforming the theatre into a
world and obliterating the bounds of time and space. To achieve
this calls for the actors' skill and the audience's attention, but it
calls for more—more indeed than the somewhat passive, albeit
willing, suspension of disbelief for the moment. It calls for the
active stirring of the imagination, that force of the mind that
moves beyond fact and reason. It calls indeed for the play of that
faculty of which Burton said—in the passage already quoted—
'In time of sleep [it] is free, and many times conceives strange,
stupend, absurd shapes . . .' In short, it calls us to a kind of dream.
As the suspension of the control of reason permits the free play of
the imagination, and through it of forces in our natures that lie
deep and often unacknowledged, so the relaxation of that control
in the theatre and the stirring of the imagination enable those same
forces to be touched, under the guidance of the art of playwright
and actors. Any play, then, bears that much resemblance to a dream.
When the play itself is presented as a dream, the effect is heightened.

And so we are brought back to the play that is our principal
object of discussion. The first thing to be said about *A Midsummer
Night's Dream* is that it is a dream—perhaps the first dream play

7

in the language. If the title leaves us in any doubt, then surely Puck's epilogue must dispel it:

> If we shadows have offended,
> Think but this, and all is mended,
> That you have but slumbered here,
> While these visions did appear.
> And this weak and idle theme,
> No more yielding but a dream,
> Gentles, do not reprehend.

It was not unusual for an actor to address an appeal to the audience at the end of a play, but this is a quaintly protective one. Up to the time when he wrote this play, Shakespeare had stayed pretty well within the bounds of sure theatrical practice: the traditions of history, the secure lines of Roman farce, classical debate, even Senecan horrors. But his art was carrying him forward into new territory. Now he was to give a far freer rein to his fantasy and to make correspondingly greater demands on that of his audience. The drama is the riskiest of the arts, and to bring in, God shield us, a new kind of creation, a lion among ladies, was a most dreadful thing. But in a dream all things are possible. What member of any audience has not known in dreams the terrors and the joys, the pursuits and despairs, of a wood near Athens? Have we not all seen strange creatures, with something of the supernatural about them, that can sleep in a cowslip yet speak with our voices, move with our motion—though freer and lovelier? Have we not seen strange, stupend, absurd shapes—part human, part asinine, perhaps? Have we not known time and nature to be confounded, so that what is announced as a four days' action turns out to be the work of two or three, and though we are told that the old moon has almost done waning—surely the time when nights are darkest—we move almost at once to a wood steeped in moonlight? Add to the magic of the theatre the magical possibilities of the dream, and all is mended.

Perhaps something else also prompted him. In his early years in the theatre, he must have seen often enough how the finest moments intended by the artist may be frustrated by uncomprehending actors or an unsympathetic audience or the sheer limitations and intransigence of the physical theatre. Confronted by these, what could the artist do but either abandon his art because it could never reach that perfection of expression that its creator, solitary and hidden in the light of thought, intended, never match

8

the dream that gave rise to it—or accept the hazards and the limitations, knowing that the perfection of expression might occur only most rarely, if at all?

> Between the conception
> And the creation
> Between the emotion
> And the response
> Falls the Shadow

Eliot is not here using the word 'Shadow' in the Shakespearian sense to which I have referred; his comment is no less suggestive on that account. Bully Bottom, who was himself something of an actor, and of a director and playwright as well, discovered the problem:

> I have had a most rare vision. I have had a dream, past the wit of man to say what dream it was. Man is but an ass, if he go about to expound this dream. Methought I was—there is no man can tell what. Methought I had—but man is but a patched fool, if he will offer to say, what methought I had. The eye of man hath not heard, the ear of man hath not seen, man's hand is not able to taste, his tongue to conceive, nor his heart to report, what my dream was.

Bottom's instinct is totally right: only through the ways of art can this thing be made plain, if at all. He will therefore get Peter Quince to write a ballad of it.

What Bottom has discovered is the problem of the artist in any age. Three centuries later, Joseph Conrad's Marlow was to restate it in the greatest of English short stories:

> It seems to me that I am trying to tell you a dream—making a vain attempt, because no relation of a dream can convey the dream-sensation, that commingling of absurdity, surprise, and bewilderment in a tremor of struggling revolt, that notion of being captured by the incredible which is of the very essence of dreams. . . . No, it is impossible; it is impossible to convey the life-sensation of any given epoch of one's existence—that which makes its truth, its meaning—its subtle and penetrating essence. It is impossible. We live, as we dream—alone . . .

Marlow has carried the statement a step farther than Bottom: it is not the artist only who moves through life in deep, essential solitude. It is Everyman. We all move in incommunicable dreams,

9

nor will any amount of twentieth-century claptrap about turning the world into a global village alter the fact. It is a condition of individual life, and it leads directly to the trite but inevitable reflection that not only is every man an island—whatever his connection with the main may be—but he is also an actor. It is hardly surprising that in the same year that Shakespeare wrote the prologue to *Henry V,* appealing to his audience to work through their imaginations at turning the stage into a world, he should have written Jaques's speech on the theme that all the world's a stage. The thought seems never to have been far from his consciousness. Lear learns to accept his humanity and that of others and to be reconciled with the fact that

> When we are born, we cry that we are come
> To this great stage of fools.

Macbeth, unreconciled and despairing, finds life to be but a walking shadow, a poor player.

What takes place, then, in this dream in which we are invited to participate—this dream of a midsummer night? For every dream has its action and atmosphere, and when we try to describe them we inevitably find ourselves telling a story—selecting materials and arranging them. Even the writing of history is, as Frank Kermode has remarked, the imposition of a plot on time. And when Shakespeare sets the dream before us, he does so with supreme artistry.

The setting is, for one of his plays, surprisingly simple, achieving indeed that classical unity of place that he was ordinarily quite content to ignore. There is a single scene at the court of Theseus, followed by one at Quince's house; then we are taken to the wood for the central action; from it we return first to Quince's house, then to the court of Theseus for the final act. The court, then, provides the outer frame of the story. It is a place where a certain social formality, the restraints of government and law, of property and age, are in force. The wood, where the story has its dark yet moonlit centre, knows nothing of such human authority. We are deeper in a dream where there are beings that resemble us, yet move with freedom that is denied us and possess powers that we do not have, where passions shift abruptly in both quality and focus, where the human may take on the subhuman and grotesque, where what happens has more of both delight and despair than our waking reason commonly admits, where the impossible is commonplace. Between the court and the wood is the house of Snug, where a group of unlettered artisans wrestle with the practical problems of stage production, in the hope of pleasing the duke.

This duke, although he presides over the main action of the play, is not one of Shakespeare's courtly heroes. He is of course too self-regarding to remind the court—as the fairies presently remind us—that he is a veteran of violence, for whom rape is neither unfamiliar nor much regretted. On the other hand, he is not so tactful as to avoid reminding Hippolyta that he wooed her with his sword, or later to tell her rather ungallantly that the lover who thinks his beloved supremely attractive is only imagining things: seeing Helen's beauty in a brow of Egypt. Small wonder if Hippolyta should appear a somewhat cool, perhaps even a trifle reluctant, bride.

In fact there is no heroic figure in the play, nor does Shakespeare here seem much interested in that exploration of character that has been the chief object of admiration and comment by generations of critics. Demetrius is hardly distinguishable from Lysander, Helena from Hermia. Bottom stands out among the mechanicals, and is indeed one of Shakespeare's great comic creations, as John Palmer has argued at length. But the play does not focus mainly on him, however much he would have liked it to do so.

There remain the fairies. They are by no means the harmlessly playful sprites that we might like to think. Puck introduces us to his merry pranks and jests; but when Oberon and Titania appear, they continue a long-standing quarrel, and what they say reveals themselves and increases our knowledge of Theseus and Hippolyta:

OBERON: Tarry, rash wanton. Am not I thy lord?

TITANIA: Then I must be thy lady. But I know
When thou hast stolen away from fairyland,
And in the shape of Corin sat all day,
Playing on pipes of corn, and versing love
To amorous Phyllida. Why art thou here
Come from the furthest steep of India?
But that, forsooth, the bouncing Amazon,
Your buskined mistress, and your warrior love,
To Theseus must be wedded; and you come,
To give their bed joy and prosperity.

OBERON: How canst thou thus, for shame, Titania,
Glance at my credit with Hippolyta,
Knowing I know thy love to Theseus?
Didst thou not lead him through the glimmering night

From Perigenia, whom he ravished?
And make him with fair Aegles break his faith,
With Ariadne, and Antiopa?

TITANIA: These are the forgeries of jealousy.
And never, since the middle summer's spring,
Met we on hill, in dale, forest, or mead,
By paved fountain, or by rushy brook,
Or in the beached margent of the sea,
To dance our ringlets with the whistling wind,
But with thy brawls thou hast disturbed our sport.
Therefore the winds, piping to us in vain,
As in revenge, have sucked up from the sea
Contagious fogs; which falling in the land,
Hath every pelting river made so proud,
That they have overborne their continents.
The ox hath therefore stretched his yoke in vain,
The plowman lost his sweat, and the green corn
Hath rotted ere his youth attained a beard.
The fold stands empty in the drowned field,
The crows are fatted with the murrion flock;
The nine-men's-morris is filled up with mud
And the quaint mazes in the wanton green
For lack of tread are indistinguishable.
The human mortals want their winter cheer,
No night is now with hymn or carol blest.

And so on. The description is not unlike that that Shakespeare was
to give, through the mouth of the duke of Burgundy, of the effects
of war on the fertile landscape of France in the time of Henry V.
Certainly if you and I as spectators are the dreamers of this dream,
the creatures that speak in this way come from depths in our
natures where there is more of wanton destructiveness, sensuality
and malevolence than was to be captured by the dainty music of
Mendelssohn or, I suspect, the voices of children. This is not to
say that the fairies are harmful only. They may and do act so as to
benefit certain human beings; but when they do, it is by caprice,
not through any general concern for the happiness of mankind.

In a description of the 1960 Aldeburgh Festival production of
Benjamin Britten's operatic version of this play, W. M. Merchant
writes as follows:

From the first Britten had noted the dark undertones of the
play: 'The fairies are very different from the innocent nothings

that often appear in productions of Shakespeare. I have always been struck by a kind of sharpness in Shakespeare's fairies.' This quality is realized in Piper's settings. They have a dark, almost sub-marine quality, with a disconcerting trick of shifting scale and proportion; a flower suddenly takes on the giant dimensions of a tree . . . so that lovers and rustics are dwarfed by a dandelion head; fairies at a turn of lighting are momentarily revealed as of oak-like proportions. As gauze after gauze was drawn, plane after plane of the vision world came into focus and then receded; the whole production, in music and setting, had at once the frightening clarity of a nightmare and the blurred edges of a dream.

When the action of the play begins, the court of Theseus, despite the approaching marriage, is a scene of division and disharmony. Hermia is defying the authority of her father. She and Lysander are both confronted by the harsh effect of the law, which, rigidly interpreted by Theseus, will force division on them. Demetrius is set against them by love and jealousy. Helena's lifelong friendship with Hermia is threatened by the same forces.

When next we see these four they have fled, variously motivated, to the wood—shadowy, but lit by the moon, the timeless friend of lovers and madmen. In the scenes that follow, Shakespeare guides them through a spirited romp, and by the mistakes of Puck rings the changes on their theoretically possible relationships. As he had multiplied the complexities and therefore the fun of *A Comedy of Errors* by doubling the number of twins he found in Plautus' play, so here he increases the comic complications over what he had introduced by the same device in *The Two Gentlemen of Verona.* If in our laughter we dismiss what happens as quite absurd, we might remember that Iris Murdoch has managed a somewhat similar piece of business in *A Severed Head,* with no fewer than six lovers. It is true that the dark wood of her novel is the city of London, and Puck is replaced by a psychiatrist. We may even wish to speculate about what may happen to Shakespeare's reputation when psychiatrists rediscover fairies. Indeed, much of what I have been saying about *A Midsummer Night's Dream* suggests a pattern familiar enough to followers of C. G. Jung, and I find it curious that Jung himself seems never to have discussed this play.

At all events, the four young Athenians, through a long night of flight and pursuit, of sudden changes of fortune and affection, delight and despair, seek what all lovers seek: the assurance, through the promise of sexual union, of love fulfilled and of the possibility of tranquillity in a world of doubt, terror and ultimate solitude. These things the civil, restricted world of the court denied them; they find them in the darkness of the uncultivated wood. What they could not find in the structured, rationalized life of society, they find in the life of imagination—sacred to the lunatic, the lover and the poet.

That we are never seriously worried about them but, on the contrary, laugh at the pattern of shifting affections that they weave, matters little. Shakespeare has been careful not to develop their personalities to a point where we are deeply concerned for them, and we are never in serious doubt about the outcome. Or is our laughter in part a measure of our own feeling of twentieth-century superiority and sophistication—this being the age of flower-power and the love-in? Does it express our middle-aged worldly-wisdom, our jaded recognition that young love has always been like this and that the lovers will get over it without anyone's being the worse? For when the lovers return to the life of the court, having found that reassurance that they so desperately sought, it is not long before they are themselves mocking at the performance of a story of young lovers separated by a wall that their fathers have built and seeking each other in a place of darkness and fear—though the moon shines with a good grace. Perhaps their merriment and ours is directed mainly at Bottom and his fellows rather than at Pyramus and Thisbe; but it is hardly plausible that Shakespeare, writing this sequence of laughter, was not thinking of that other moonlit play, so nearly contemporary with this one, in which two lovers separated by parental broils seek each other in death at a place of death. We are entitled to ask whether the laughter of the four young lovers at the court of Theseus would not have had a very different quality if they had not experienced their night in the wood.

Into the wood also come the members of the Athens Little Theatre Society to rehearse their play. They are of course the proper objects of our laughter. All the same, we should note that their principal concern has to do precisely with the problem of imagination. They are totally unsophisticated about it—simultaneously afraid of stimulating it too vigorously and of trusting to its own force. The introduction of an unprologued lion will be as great a threat to their play as the failure to indicate that the moon is shining by introducing a suitably garbed actor. How marvellously right that Bully Bottom, the person most concerned about this problem and most resourceful in dealing with it, is

14

precisely the one to whom it is given to discover most deeply the indescribable wonder of a dream!

Division and dissension are, as we have noted, not confined to members of the court of Theseus. The rulers of fairyland have quarrelled, and for them too this night in the wood is to be a time when they become reconciled, rediscovering mutual affection and tranquillity. If the reconciliation is effected through the superior trickery of Oberon, the parallel is all the closer: Theseus has no compunction about having won Hippolyta by doing her injuries.

Nor is it only Bottom who, as daylight breaks, is conscious of the dreamlike quality of the experience that he has had. Titania comes to herself with the words,

> My Oberon, what visions have I seen!

And the four human lovers, after they have—with a certain understandable sheepishness—explained to Theseus the reorganization of their relationships, talk with wonder among themselves:

DEMETRIUS: These things seem small and undistinguishable,
Like far-off mountains turned into clouds.

HERMIA: Methinks I see these things with parted eye,
When everything seems double.

HELENA: So methinks.
And I have found Demetrius, like a jewel,
Mine own, and not mine own.

DEMETRIUS: Are you sure
That we are awake? It seems to me
That yet we sleep, we dream. Do not you think
The Duke was here, and bid us follow him?

HERMIA: Yea, and my father.

HELENA: And Hippolyta.

LYSANDER: And he did bid us follow to the temple.

DEMETRIUS: Why then we are awake; let's follow him,
And by the way let us account our dreams.

Shakespeare's fondness for introducing a play within his play is familiar enough. Here we have dreams within a dream—followed in due course by the play within the play. It seems to

15

me that in *A Midsummer Night's Dream* for the first time—and never again with the same union of richness and delicacy—Shakespeare obtains that astonishing effect of unsounded depths, of varying and intermingling planes of experience, of multiplicity of meanings, that is most peculiarly his own. If the presence of an audience on the stage (whether at the court of Theseus or of Claudius of Denmark) reminds us that we also are not only members of an audience but actors on a stage, does not the presence of dreamers within this dream remind us freshly—after Puck has awakened us—of the dreamlike character of the 'real' life to which we return from the theatre? Our minds go forward to the masque that is presented before Prospero's cell, and the moment when Prospero, dismissing his actors into the thin air from which they came, reminds his audience on the stage, and therefore the audience in the theatre, that

> We are such stuff
> As dreams are made on, and our little life
> Is rounded with a sleep.

'A man that is born falls into a dream like a man who falls into the sea,' says one of Joseph Conrad's characters.

At the end of Act IV of our play, the pattern of romantic comedy that Shakespeare was to follow repeatedly was practically complete. That pattern involves a court—of Athens or Illyria, Duke Senior or Milan—a place of civility and authority where nevertheless dissension has arisen. There are several pairs of lovers, separated from one another and made solitary by the opposition of parents or the cruel perversity of laws of man or nature. There is a period of isolation when the lovers seek one another—in the depths of a forest, the secrecy of disguise or the darkness of their own beings. Then comes the time of discoveries, followed by the reconstitution of the court, the return from solitude to society, from delusion to truth, the rightings of wrongs, the reconciliation of differences. Always there is a pervasive sense of uncertainty, for what can these multiple disguises, mistaken identities, shifting affections, the endless playing with words and images, do but remind us of the dreamlike quality of what we call 'real' life, even as we are carried through a pattern that terminates in reconciliation and the affirmation of life's joy? The scenes in the wood, in *A Midsummer's Night's Dream,* make this effect more explicit by making it clear that it is precisely out of what is most dreamlike that what is most substantial emerges—Hippolyta calls it 'something of great constancy'. We may find ourselves thinking of Shakespeare's use of the same paradox in *Lear*.

The dreams within the dream are followed by the play within the play. We have returned to the court of Theseus. A triple wedding has taken place, a night of triple consummation will follow. Meanwhile, it is a time for festivity, for laughter, for dancing, for high spirits, good fellowship and the celebration of the joys of the earth. Every lover has his lass. Bully Bottom and his friends have their triumph. Even that ever-present menace, the generation gap, is forgotten; for surely, though Shakespeare makes no mention of the fact, the crotchety Egeus must join in the merry-making.

We ought to note one point in relation to this scene of merriment. I have mentioned *Romeo and Juliet* in connection with *Pyramus and Thisbe*. Critics have made the comment from time to time that *Romeo and Juliet*, up to the end of Act IV, follows (except for certain stark episodes and the generally ominous atmosphere) the pattern of Shakespearian romantic comedy as I have described it. It is only Romeo's exclamation when he receives the mistaken message—'Is it even so? Then I defy you, stars'—that plunges us surely into the darkness of tragedy. The pattern that could so easily have led to the comic conclusion, with its richness of love and reconciliation and the promise of life, leads instead through pain and violence to the final solitude of death. For death *is* the final solitude, as almost every Shakespearian tragedy makes plain. Only for Mark Antony and Cleopatra, for whom there awaits an eternity of love-making in Elysian fields, is it anything else.

I think it is for this reason that *Pyramus and Thisbe* provides so apt a vehicle of celebration in the fifth act of *A Midsummer Night's Dream*. There has been one moment during the night in the woods when death seemed ready to look in, and but for the interposition of Puck, might have done so. Now, when the note of reconciliation, of love and life, must be struck, that thought of the nearness of death must be exorcised. With the riotous buffoonery of *Pyramus and Thisbe* as played by Bottom and Company, the exorcism occurs. So against uncertainty and fear, darkness and solitude and death, are set beauty and love, feasting and companionship and the affirmation of life. They are so woven together that for some golden moments we are allowed to believe that they will remain. The pattern of comic reassurance, as B. H. Lehman has called it, is made secure.

But never quite secure. In the final chord of Shakespearian comedy there is always a minor note. However lightly touched,

17

it is insistent, reminding the listener that the joy has come out of distress and that the alloy of pain or solitude is never finally removed. As the richest of the comedies ends, that eternal separatist Malvolio stalks off, vowing revenge; and at the last Feste remains alone on the stage to sing about the wind and the rain, those daily reminders of human vulnerability.

That minor note is struck in *A Midsummer Night's Dream* also. As midnight sounds, Theseus breaks in on the revels:

> Lovers, to bed, 'tis almost fairy time.

He speaks playfully; perhaps, in view of what we have seen of him, mockingly. Yet he reminds us that the powers of night are lurking. And although they may at the moment be only benevolent towards the lovers, Puck nonetheless reminds us that the hungry lion roars and the wolf behowls the moon:

> Now it is the time of night,
> That the graves, all gaping wide,
> Every one lets forth his sprite,
> In the church-way paths to glide.

If now we have followed the course of this play, have yielded ourselves to its delight, we shall find the pattern of comedy has worked its effect. We shall, I take it, emerge from the theatre with a renewed sense of the possibility of delight in life and its source in human relations, and of the transitoriness and uncertainty that continually veil it from us. If a comedy does this richly, what more ought we to ask?

Still, it seems to me that *A Midsummer Night's Dream* does something more. If we now recall what I have said about Shakespeare's concern with the imagination and his awareness of the theatre as a world and the world as a stage, we may, I think, perceive what it conveys—and conveys better than any other of the comedies before *The Tempest*. As the lovers go into the forest, and searching in its darkness and mystery find light and stability, an experience so profound for them that Hippolyta refers to it as a kind of transfiguration, so we, the audience, are invited to participate in a dream, an act of the imagination. Allowing the forces of the poet's mind and the actors' skill to work their way with us, we also may participate in the transfiguration—suffer a sea change, if you like, and if the sea happens to be a wood near Athens, it matters little. This, it seems to me, is the invitation and the challenge of this play and indeed of all great art. The presentation of it here is perhaps the surest indication that Shakespeare had reached that richly mature condition that Keats was to call Negative Capability. The truth that he deals in is imaginative and artistic truth; he is little concerned with the irritable reaching after fact and reason.

In the world that we re-enter when we leave the theatre, the forces of what we are pleased to call 'real' life close around us again, and the irritable reaching after fact and reason is waiting to be resumed. The terrible impulsion to measure everything is not likely to go away, nor can we count on having enough people like E. E. Cummings, to remind us passionately,

(While you and i have lips and voices which
are for kissing and to sing with,
who cares if some oneeyed son of a bitch
invents an instrument to measure Spring with?

Our transfigurations will not come by means of computers or radioactive carbon, any more than by observing the vagaries of the gross national product. The fact, as Matthew Arnold noted a century ago, continues to fail us.

Lest I be misunderstood, let me give the second last word to a scientist. Many years ago a German chemist had a dream. He had been working for a long time at the problem of finding a graphic means of representing the molecular structure of a certain compound. In his dream he saw the formulae with which he had been working begin to take the form of strange, frightening, snakelike creatures, twisting and moving fantastically. Suddenly one of these snakes got hold of its own tail and—as he described it later—'the whole structure was mockingly twisting in front of my eyes.' The solution to his problem was there: he awoke, and wrote down in effect a circular formula instead of a linear one. Reporting his discovery subsequently, he admonished his fellow-scientists: 'Let us learn to dream, gentlemen, and then we may perhaps find the truth.'

The truth he had discovered was of a more utilitarian order than imaginative and artistic truth generally is. Its ways in ordering our experience and our feelings, and indeed those forces in our natures that are beyond the comprehension of reason, are likely to be both more subtly indirect and more personal. Let me then give the last word to Hippolyta, for she understood this. When she has listened to the story of the lovers' adventures in the woods and heard out the sceptical Theseus on the subject, she states her view that something more has been at work than can be defined by such terms as fancy and imagination—something not wonderful only, but deeply creative:

> But all the story of the night told over,
> And all their minds transfigured so together,
> More witnesseth than fancy's images,
> And grows to something of great constancy;
> But howsoever, strange and admirable.

MEASURE FOR MEASURE: A COMEDY

Geoffrey Durrant

In attempting to understand *Measure for Measure*, we must first of all recognize that the task will not be easy. This play, in common with *Troilus and Cressida, Hamlet* and *All's Well that Ends Well*, has been classified by some of the most respected of Shakespearians as a 'problem play'—a term that is conveniently ambiguous, since it leaves us free to suppose that the play was a problem to Shakespeare, or to his audience or is merely one for ourselves. It may moreover be taken to mean that the difficulties we experience with the play are to be explained on the grounds that Shakespeare, when he wrote it, was undergoing a spiritual or psychological crisis that expresses itself in the confusion of an unsatisfactory play—a morbid or savage expression of an inner turmoil.

Any one of these explanations may be right. However, we must note that academic criticism has a habit of creating categories in which it subsequently finds itself trapped. A case in point is the elaboration by the followers of Bradley of a theory of tragedy derived from Aristotle, complete with tragic inevitability, tragic flaw, purgation and character analysis. Although this scheme works well enough not to seem flagrantly wrong when it is applied to *King Lear, Macbeth* or *Coriolanus* it runs into difficulties with *Hamlet,* and it may be seen tying itself in its own knots when it is applied to the *Excellent and Lamentable Tragedie of Romeo and Juliet*. Of this play the Bradleians have told us that it is a comparative failure. It does not depend on tragic inevitability, but on bad luck; the hero is not a 'representative figure', but an ordinary young man; there are patches of less than tragic verse; we do not experience the tragic purgation. The conclusion to be drawn, it seems, is not that the theory is wrong, or wrongly applied to this play, but that Shakespeare failed. At best he is to be given an alpha minus, some of which is for Effort; he was after all, as we are told, trying his 'prentice hand'. The generations of playgoers and readers who have found no difficulty with the play and who have understood it, as Coleridge did, as a dramatic love-poem with an unhappy ending have been, according to much of the academic criticism of this century, simply uninformed. They have not eat paper, they have not drunk ink; their intellect is not replenished.

In inviting you to take systematic theories of Tragedy and of Comedy, when applied to the work of Shakespeare, with some scepticism, I do not wish to assert that we should be indifferent to the simpler distinctions between comedy and tragedy. On the contrary, I think it is clear that these distinctions are radically important. Charlie Chaplin asserted this indirectly when he said, as he is reported to have said, 'Comedy is made with long-shots; tragedy with close-ups'—a remark that contains more good sense than whole volumes of Aristotelian system-making. When Shakespeare's friends and editors published his collected works, they separated Tragedies, Comedies and Histories. On the whole, it seems, we can safely say that tragedies usually end unhappily, comedies end happily and histories end as history dictates, neither happily nor unhappily. We may also note that although each comedy is given only its individual title, each tragedy is also described explicitly as a tragedy—*The Tragedie of King Lear, The Tragedie of Julius Caesar* and so on. The exception in the folio is the story of Timon of Athens, which is described only as his 'Life'. We must also note that a play that ends happily—*Cymbeline* —is included among the tragedies and is entitled *The Tragedie of Cymbeline.* For Shakespeare's friends and contemporaries, 'tragedy' evidently did not mean what it meant for the followers of Bradley. Usually it was applied to a play with an unhappy ending, but one play at least with a happy ending qualified to be called a 'tragedy'.

If you ask me what I want to make of all this, the answer is 'not very much'. I want only to assert that Shakespeare's first editors, who knew the conditions of his theatre and knew what the audience would expect, themselves thought that it was important to label certain plays as tragedies, so that the reader would know what he was to be let in for. These are in general plays that end unhappily, for such plays will call for an effort of sympathy, will not afford us the pleasures of detached amusement and will therefore not be suitable fare when we want chiefly relaxation. This may then be understood as a *caveat lector,* a warning to brace ourselves for a commitment of deep human sympathy. The two exceptions in the folio, *Timon of Athens* and *Cymbeline,* tend on the whole to confirm this suggestion. *Timon of Athens* is included with the tragedies, but is not called a 'tragedy'; it asks us to contemplate the bitterness of Timon's existence, but it makes little appeal to our active human sympathies. *Cymbeline* is both classified and named as a 'tragedy', although it ends happily. It is however unusual among plays that end happily in making a strong demand on our sympathy with a man caught in remorse and despair and undergoing a spiritual purgation. In other words, it calls on our feelings of the common human fate to the point of demanding a certain *awe,* a metaphysical or religious feeling, a sense that Posthumus represents our own sinful condition. In contemplating his anguish, we may not permit ourselves the pleasure of detached criticism; we are not allowed to say to ourselves, 'What a fool!' and laugh our way out of our painful sympathy with him.

This then I believe to be the really important distinction between a comedy and a tragedy. It lies in the approach we are invited to make to the events on the stage. If we know from the beginning that the chief actor is doomed, either to actual death or to the kind of anguish experienced by Posthumus (which is nothing less than the death of his old self), we are not free to be amused, to laugh, except in parenthetical passages of subplot which serve to relax us for the next turn of the screw. The gladiators of ancient Rome, before a fight to the death, greeted the emperor with 'Morituri te salutant'—'Those about to die, salute thee!' It is hard to believe that any but the most depraved of spectators could laugh, after that, at a swordsman caught in the net of the retiarius. Nor do we have any tendency to laughter, except in the most outrageously bad production, when Lear is behaving in a very silly way. He would be a ridiculous old man if he were not about to die. So the distinction between tragedy and comedy is both simple and fundamental. Tragedies are made with 'close-ups'—with human sympathy and with religious awe, in the face of the ultimate human vulnerability. Comedies are made with 'long-shots'—with a detached, critical, amused view of the human absurdities performed before us. We may so indulge ourselves because we are given a kind of guarantee by the playwright that the persons we smile at are not going to suffer anything very serious. A comedy is a play that begins like a comedy, lets us know that we are free to laugh, gives us occasion for laughter or for smiles and duly arrives at a happy ending. An unhappy ending to *Much Ado about Nothing* or to *Twelfth Night* is inconceivable; the audience would feel that it had been tricked into a breach of that decorum of feeling which all men observe in the face of the ultimate human agonies. In this respect a comedy resembles a fairy tale; just as children are reassured by the familiar 'once upon a time' at the beginning of a fairy tale and confidently look forward to 'lived happily ever after', the audience watches the beginning of a play (or the playbill) to discover whether this is to be a story with a happy or an unhappy ending. The whole mode of our response depends upon this very simple but necessary decorum of feeling.

If we turn now to *Measure for Measure* with these considerations in mind, they may suggest an answer to the problems over which so many critics disagree. Is this a funny play, or a 'bitter' one, a satire, or a tragi-comedy? Is Isabella a saintly heroine, or a prig? What is the role of the duke, who appears as a god from the machine whenever the plot needs a little help? Why does Shakespeare, if this is a deeply serious and even solemn play, allow Isabella to play the bawd to Mariana?

I suggest that a possible answer lies in the nature of *Measure for Measure* as a comedy—as a play that we know from the start is going to end happily. For if this is clearly established early in the play, we are relieved of that emotional decorum which forbids us to laugh at saints, to smile at death, to be amused by executions. For this is a saint who is going, in some way or other (in accordance with the conventions of comedy) to make a good marriage, as do all heroines in comedy. The deaths that seem to be imminent are not going to happen; the executions will be play-acting; the injustice from the very beginning foreseen, provided for, out-generalled and corrected. If this is so, we may freely smile or even laugh at themes which in real life we may only contemplate with due solemnity. In real life, where there is no all-controlling duke, we do not permit ourselves to laugh at prostitution, injustice, cruelty, lust and hatred of life; perhaps we dare not, and certainly we feel we must not. In this way we lose one of the weapons we might employ against these evils; we deny ourselves the recognition of their silliness. My claim for *Measure for Measure* is that it achieves to an exceptional degree the liberation—possible only in a fictional world—of laughter (rather than indignation) in the face of moral and social evil. This I believe to be the source of the unique achievement of this play, and also of the bewilderment it has caused the critics.

It will not do to say simply that Shakespeare took over the un-satisfactory or difficult parts of his story from his source in Whet-stone's two 'Comical Discourses' of Promos and Cassandra, based on Cinthio. He did after all choose to use this source and set to work, we must suppose, to make the story into an acceptable play. Michelangelo declares in a sonnet that the best of artists has no idea ('concetto') that he does not find hidden in the marble with

which he is working. In the same way, we may accept that Shakespeare took much from his sources, but what he found in them was usually a challenge to an achievement which in each case transcends the source itself. As with the knots in wood or the veins in marble worked on by the sculptor, the dramatic artist is offered, by the difficulties of the story he works with, an opportunity to exercise his art by turning even improbabilities, absurdities and crudities into elements in a unified account of human life. Nothing that we know of Shakespeare's art authorizes us to take the easy way out and explain our own disagreements or bewilderments in the case of any particular play in terms of Shakespeare's unsuccessful struggle with difficult material, for after all the material was of his own choosing. Also, the changes made by Shakespeare in the story serve to emphasize the artificiality of the plot by giving a more continuous and important share of the action to the god from the machine. It is Shakespeare, moreover, who makes the heroine refuse to sacrifice her chastity and protect her own virtue by substituting Mariana, for whom there is no equivalent in the earlier versions of the story. There can be no question of a slavish adherence by Shakespeare to unsatisfactory features of the story he chose to adapt. On the contrary, it seems more profitable to treat these changes as offering us some hints of Shakespeare's intentions, which seem to have been to increase the controlled improbability of the story and to expose the heroine to critical and even, as Professor Clifford Leech suggests, 'clinical' examination.

In suggesting that *Measure for Measure,* in spite of subject matter that seems to call for solemn consideration, invites us to the response that we give characteristically to comedy, I do not wish to deny the 'disturbing' nature of the material it includes. Human self-centredness, self-righteousness, injustice, the terror of death, prostitution, guilt, are presented in this play without any flinching from their true nature. What I wish to assert, however, is that there is no material that by its nature is unsuitable for contemplation in the spirit of comedy, and that it is Shakespeare's achievement, in this play, to have offered us the liberation of a comic view of some of the more frightening and disturbing aspects of our common human nature. Only those who confuse solemnity with seriousness will suppose that a critical and comic view is inappropriate when disturbing topics are presented.

This comic liberation, I suggest, is prepared for by our recognition, early in the play, that this is a comedy and that it will end happily—as comedies are expected to end—with forgiveness all round and the marriage of the heroine. (All Shakespeare's comedies

25

end in marriage or the restoration of a marriage.) It is furthered also by the deliberate use of a god from the machine who clearly has the whole situation under control and who offers an unusual under-pinning of the comic reassurance, both by his statement of the terms of the experiment and by his constant reappearances. It is also furthered by the additional improbabilities introduced by Shakespeare into the story, which increase the sense we have of observing an elaborate experiment. Finally the comic liberation —the permission to smile—is paradoxically offered by the religious overtones of the play, and in particular by the duke's speech, as a friar, on the nothingness of human existence. All these work together to give to the audience a detachment incompatible with the tragic mode, but friendly to the spirit of comedy.

The reassurance provided by the controlling presence of the duke is, I suggest, an important source of the freedom we enjoy from anxious human sympathy. By itself, however, it could scarcely suffice to carry us through the pitiful spectacle of Claudio yielding to the fear of death, or the grim insensibility of Barnadine, and the attendant jesting:

> Pray, Master Barnadine, awake till you are executed, and
> sleep afterwards.

Shakespeare however provides, in the ministrations of the duke as a friar to Claudio, a speech which serves to place the audience at some distance, not only from the events on the stage, but from all the concerns of human kind. Before the most distressing scene in the play Shakespeare gives to the duke a lengthy speech that sets all human life and the agony of death in a context of religious detachment. From the friar's point of view, it is mere foolishness to attach so much anxiety and fear to human fate:

> . . . Reason thus with life:
> If I do lose thee, I do lose a thing
> That none but fools would keep: a breath thou art,
> (Servile to all the skyey influences,)
> That dost this habitation where thou keep'st
> Hourly afflict: merely, thou art death's fool.

> . . . . Thou hast nor youth nor age,
> But, as it were, an after-dinner's sleep,
> Dreaming on both.

We need not suppose that this represents Shakespeare's view of life. The function of the speech in the play seems to be to set the concerns of the human beings in it in a context of religious thought, thus reducing human anguish to the status of a merely temporary condition and making death itself into a release. After this speech it is easier to observe Claudio's anguished fear of death with a certain detachment and to find something funny—without any gross emotional indecorum—even in the grim jests about Barnadine's execution. The god from the machine not only provides us with the assurance that he will not let anything disastrous occur; he also asks us, in poetry that exerts a strong persuasion over us, whether it would very much matter, after all, if the 'worst' did happen to Claudio, Barnadine, or Isabella. This I take not as moral nihilism in Shakespeare, but as a necessary pre-condition for taking a comic view of the otherwise disturbing scenes that follow.

The very first scene of the play shows us the careful erection of a safety net which will allow us to watch the antics of the personages on the stage without any imaginative fear that anybody will break his neck. The duke is represented as making a controlled experiment with a carefully chosen subject—Angelo. The object of the experiment is to find out how he will survive the test of power:

What figure of us, think you, he will bear?

When Angelo duly appears, the terms of the experiment are set out clearly: the test of virtue is in action, and it is to the crucial test of opportunity that Angelo's famous virtues are now to be subjected. Even Angelo knows that this is a risky experiment and begs that there may be some more trial made of his 'mettle' before the test of supreme responsibility is applied. The next scenes reveal just how dangerous the experiment would be if it were not strictly controlled by the duke from behind the scenes; Angelo is already trying to cure immorality with law, which makes no distinction between lechery and the merely technical fornication of Claudio and Juliet. In Act I, Scene iv, however, any fears we may have had that things will turn out disastrously are removed. The duke is not going away; he is on the spot disguised as a friar. Since the experiment, as the duke tells us, will show 'what our seemers be', we know that the duke is prepared to deal with Angelo's aberrations. The god from the machine is ready to control everything, and this continual observation and intervention by a benevolent power, far from representing a defect in the play, is the condition of its special achievement. It is through the reassurance the duke provides that we are left free to laugh at both the 'seemer' and his victims, since we know that no lasting harm will come to anybody. Moreover, the reappearances of the god from the machine provide the audience with constant reminders that nobody will come to harm, and so enable Shakespeare to achieve comic effects of an unusual kind and with most unusual materials.

The use that Shakespeare makes of this freedom appears most plainly when we first meet Isabella. How are we to take her first words to the nun who is to admit her to the sisterhood of Saint Clare? She asks about the sisters' privileges, and seems to know their business better than they do:

> I speak not as desiring more,
> But rather wishing a more strict restraint
> Upon the sisterhood, the votaries of Saint Clare.

Critics inhibited by the need to feel solemn about the play will not allow themselves to see that this is a priggish remark, to be smiled at as one smiles at the earnestness of all such youthful 'idealism'. Isabella's first words have in them a touch of the solemnity that so often tinges youthful moral commitment. There is no need for a harsh judgement of her, even when she appears later in the play in an even more unflattering light. It is the perennial comedy of youth to mistake intense convictions, moral solemnity and 'commitment' for moral seriousness; and Isabella exhibits throughout the play an immaturity at which we are perhaps allowed to smile. As this is a comedy, the audience supposes that she will be married at the end of the play and that her present religious fervour and moral absolutism are not deeply engrained in her nature. A spectator considering her in the comic spirit—which includes self-criticism—may remember his own youthful moralism and self-righteousness and not treat her too censoriously. In the same way, her later failures of imagination may readily be forgiven; she is too young and inexperienced to meet in an adequately human way the moral pressures brought against her.

The discussion with Lucio that follows is crucial to the audience's view of Isabella, since in this scene we are getting to know her:

LUCIO: I would not—though it is my familiar sin
          With maids to seem the lapwing, and to jest
          Tongue far from heart—play with all virgins so:
          I hold you as a thing ensky'd and sainted;
          By your renouncement an immortal spirit;
          And to be talked with in sincerity,
          As with a saint.

ISABELLA: You do blaspheme the good in mocking me.

Lucio's praise—even if we were to take it as sincerely meant—is evidently extravagant and is received by Isabella as mockery. Dr Leavis, in his illuminating study of the play in *The Common Pursuit*, supposes that Lucio is lifted by Isabella's influence into 'a momentary state of grace' and that we are to take his tribute to her as heartfelt. It seems plain enough to me that Lucio is mocking Isabella, in spite of his protestation to the contrary; but in either case the dramatic effect is inescapably ironic. Dr Leavis notes that the exchange issues in 'a limiting and placing criticism' of Isabella, though he sees this criticism as one that the audience arrives at in the context of Lucio's uncritical admiration of her. If this scene is approached with the expectations we normally bring to comedy we are, I think, less likely to be inhibited by the religious aura of the novitiate and readier to note the mockery in Lucio's tone—a mockery entirely consistent with his behaviour throughout the play. In agreeing with Dr Leavis that a 'limiting criticism' of Isabella is inescapable, I suggest that the audience is invited, not to accept the mockery of the cynical Lucio on his own terms, but to see that Isabella is vulnerable to the comic spirit, that though we may not wish to join in Lucio's mockery, we may at least be permitted to smile at her youthful self-importance and moral earnestness. Isabella's claim that Lucio, in mocking her, is blaspheming against 'the good' is firmly rejected by Lucio: 'Do not believe it.' It is through Lucio that the audience is invited to note the difference between smiling at (or mocking) Isabella, and blaspheming. Much of the discussion of the play has been affected by the sense that we may criticize Isabella and judge her adversely, but that to smile at her would be like laughing in church—a kind of 'blaspheming'.

The comic vein is continued in the relish with which Lucio describes to the 'saintly' Isabella, on her way into the nunnery, the act of procreation of which Claudio has been guilty:

Your brother and his lover have embraced:
As those that feed grow full, as blossoming time
That from the seedness the bare fallow brings
To teeming foison, even so her plenteous womb
Expresseth his full tilth and husbandry.

Again, we do not need to admire Lucio's evident pleasure in dwelling with deliberate zest on the sexual act and its relationship to procreation; we may regard him as a profligate and cynic and still see the comedy of the imposition of the sexual theme on a young woman who at present is devoted to purity and sainthood.

The play, if it is taken from the start as comedy, offers us some assurance that Isabella is not finally destined for the convent and that her present pursuit of sanctity is not much more than youthful self-delusion and misplaced moral idealism. It is expected of nubile young women, in comedies, that they will be married at the end, and this is naturally what the audience supposes will happen to Isabella.

There is further comedy in the spectacle of Lucio urging Isabella, that model of Christian charity, to plead for her brother's life. The contrast is continued in the meeting with Angelo, where Isabella has again to be prompted by Lucio and where she is shown as dominated by the fear of seeming to condone Claudio's act of fornication. Her first words are directed to making plain her detestation of the act:

> There is a vice that most I do abhor,
> And most desire should meet the blow of justice;
> For which I would not plead, but that I must . . . (II, ii)

Isabella here is more immediately concerned for her reputation than for her brother's life. This in anything but a comedy would be painful; here, since we know that no harm will be done, we can smile at Isabella's immaturity. When Angelo refuses to relent, Isabella is horrified by the imminence of Claudio's death, chiefly on theological grounds; she has already (though only a novice) begun to take the professional view that one would expect of a nun:

> He's not prepared for death . . . even for our kitchens
> We kill the fowl of season . . . shall we serve heaven
> With less respect than we do minister
> To our gross selves?

We are free to regard this speech with moral horror, as a heartlessly abstract theological view of a brother's imminent death, or to smile at it with comic tolerance as the aberration of a pious young girl whose natural compassion and love have been sacrificed to theological abstractions during a period of religious enthusiasm. There is, it seems to me, no way of reading this application of the proper serving of poultry to the occasion of a brother's death as a fittingly serious comment by a seriously admirable young woman. In my view, the safety net that has been spread by Shakespeare under the whole action invites us to relax and ironically to smile at this youthful failure of moral imagination. This is not to say that Isabella fails to give Angelo some hard knocks in argument. She is closer to him in character than to anybody else

in the play, and there is a rich vein of comedy in her rebuking
of him for self-righteousness; it is she who expresses what I take
to be the central comic idea of the play:

> . . . Man, proud man,
> Drest in a little brief authority,
> Most ignorant of what he's most assured,
> His glassy essence—like an angry ape
> Plays such fantastic tricks before high heaven
> As makes the Angels weep . . . who with our spleens,
> Would all themselves laugh mortal.

The angels would weep, but mortals can only laugh. The laughter
is not without a touch of bitterness, but the play invites us after all
to laughter, not to a solemn contemplation of Isabella as one of
Shakespeare's more admirable young women.

Isabella's refusal to meet Angelo's demand on her needs no
defence, nor is there any need to invoke the value set on chastity
in Shakespeare's day. It is not her decision that creates discomfort
in those who might wish to see Isabella as a simply admirable
figure, but the intensely self-regarding way in which she sees the
whole situation. This appears plainly enough in the speech in
which she plans her course of action:

> I'll to my brother.
> Though he hath fallen by prompture of the blood,
> Yet hath he in him such a mind of honour,
> That had he twenty heads to tender down
> On twenty bloody blocks, he'd yield them up,
> Before his sister should her body stoop
> To such abhorr'd pollution . . .

This evidently says too much; Isabella might well hope for her
brother's willing co-operation, but to assert with so much confidence a heroism that is not hers to command suggests at least a
failure of sympathy and imagination. The 'twenty bloody blocks'
are set too lightly in the scale against the 'abhorr'd pollution'. It is
in the last words of the speech, to which the rhyme—applied not
only to the closing couplet of the scene—adds the suggestion of a
closed circle of complacent thought, that the quality of Isabella's
feeling emerges:

> Then Isabel, live chaste, and brother, die . . .
> 'More than our brother is our chastity'.
> I'll tell him yet of Angelo's request,
> And fit his mind for death, for his soul's rest.

If Shakespeare is attempting here to retain the audience's uncritical sympathy for Isabella he is evidently not doing so very successfully. It seems more reasonable to suppose that he intends a critical limitation of that sympathy. The tone is altogether too serene, the 'we' almost regal. To suppress the discomfort that this speech causes is to be intimidated by Isabella's self-confident 'virtue'; in this comedy where we need not feel any deep human sympathy for Isabella, who is plainly to come to no harm, we may allow ourselves a wry smile at her sententious readiness to claim her brother's life.

Equally, Angelo's moral anguish is ugly enough and must arouse some horror; but the horror need not be untinged with comedy; the final effect is of the grotesque, so that Angelo becomes a dramatic embodiment of the absurd delusions of the 'unco guid':

> Oh cunning enemy, that, to catch a saint,
> With saint doth bait thy hook: most dangerous
> Is that temptation that doth goad us on
> To sin, in loving virtue; never could the strumpet,
> With all her double vigour, art, and nature,
> Once stir my temper: but this virtuous maid
> Subdues me quite: ever till now
> When men were fond, I smiled, and wondered how.

Here the comedy consists in the classification of himself and Isabella as 'saints', in itself a reminder that to aim at sanctity may involve one in being less than human. Angelo's insistence that he is a *saint* (even in the manner in which he succumbs to temptation) is akin to the 'saint-like' and morally indignant air that Isabella exhibits even to a brother faced with the fear of death. The scene is crucial for the understanding of Isabella, and therefore needs some consideration.

Having decided to break the news to Claudio of the necessity of his death—a necessity which we understand from the start will not in fact operate, because of the dramatic safety net—Isabella offers to her brother what she regards, somewhat unimaginatively, as acceptable comfort; first she tells him that he is destined for heaven, and then that there is nothing to fear from the pangs of death. The illustration of the beetle at this point suggests a lack of imaginative warmth, as does the image of the preparation of a chicken for the table:

> Dar'st thou die?
> The sense of death is most in apprehension,
> And the poor beetle that we tread upon
> In corporal sufferance finds a pang as great
> As when a giant dies.

Claudio's response to Isabella's theological and physiological 'comforts' is agonized; she will not succeed in reconciling him to death by these methods, when even the duke's eloquent speech on the nothingness of human existence cannot for long subdue his sense of the value of life and of the horror of death. To speak so to him is to give him 'shame'—to fail to recognize his humanity. Isabella, with what seems needless cruelty, informs her brother that she could save his life if she would yield to Angelo; this she does immediately after he has said:

> If I must die,
> I will encounter darkness as a bride,
> And hug it in mine arms.

This mood of resolution is of course broken down by the tantalizing prospect of a reprieve at the price of his sister's honour. The dialogue that follows is crucial to an understanding of the tone of the scene:

ISABELLA: This night's the time
That I should do what I abhor to name,
Or else thou diest tomorrow.

CLAUDIO: Thou shalt not do it.

ISABELLA: O, were it but my life,
I'd throw it down for your deliverance
As frankly as a pin.

CLAUDIO: Thanks, dear Isabel.

I have been told by a student of theatre who had taken part in a production of the play that all attempts by the actors to prevent the audience from laughing outright at this point were frustrated. And in the production we saw at the Stratford Festival Theatre the audience laughed out loud at this. Was this an error on their part? A lapse of taste, a sign of insufficient reverence for the solemnities of Shakespeare's art? My own belief is that Shakespeare built this laugh into the play, that he intended it and therefore still gets it. For once we remember that Claudio is not going to die and that Isabella may keep her virtue for her husband, we are free to be amused at the earnestness of Isabella's offer of her life (when it is not in question) and at the rueful tone in which Claudio thanks her for the gratuitous offer. This is indeed to be virtuous very cheaply and with an inappropriate ostentation. The audiences who laugh at this point are to my mind better Shakespearian critics than the producers who try to lead them into a more reverent attitude.

The laughter appropriately aroused in the audience by this passage gives way to another mood, as Claudio confronts the fear of death in one of the most chilling passages in Shakespeare:

> Ay, but to die, and go we know not where,
> To lie in cold obstruction, and to rot,
> This sensible warm motion to become
> A kneaded clod, and the delighted spirit
> To bathe in fiery floods, or to reside
> In thrilling region of thick-ribbed ice . . .

This speech must move the audience to share in Claudio's fear of death; through the intensity of its poetry it reaches out beyond the confines of a comedy in which he is safe from the threat and arouses the universal *timor mortis*. Isabella's response to her brother's anguish is therefore of some importance. She might well feel pity, she might even urge her brother earnestly to remember that he could not honourably live at the cost of his sister's shame. The actual response however is shrill and indignant, untouched with pity. When in a moment of weakness he begs her to comply, she answers:

> O you beast,
> O faithless coward, O dishonest wretch,
> Wilt thou be made a man out of my vice?
> . . . . . Might but my bending down
> Reprieve thee from thy death, it should proceed.
> I'll pray a thousand prayers for thy death,
> No word to save thee.

And on his further pleading:

> O fie, fie, fie!
> Thy sin's not accidental, but a trade:
> Mercy to thee would prove itself a bawd.
> 'Tis best that thou diest quickly.

This is a disturbing scene, acceptable only as ironic dark comedy and because the presence of the duke in the background guarantees us against the full commitment of human sympathy that would be appropriate in a tragedy. At this point Shakespeare causes the duke to intervene, as if the comedy of Isabella's virtue has been taken to its limits. This permits an immediate release for Isabella from the ugly passion of self-righteous anger; even so we feel Shakespeare has put some strain on his comedy.

Isabella's detestation of the role of the bawd, proclaimed in this scene with her brother, is soon after ironically played on in her appearance at Mariana's house. The role of a go-between to bring Angelo to bed with Mariana is no more and no less sinful than the love of Claudio for Juliet, since in both cases there has been a betrothal but no marriage. It must however be remembered that Isabella has expressed to Angelo and Claudio her detestation of fornication and her contempt for the role of the bawd. However, she is easily enough prompted to a part in the plot in which the symbol of the keys—displayed to the audience by Isabella—ironically casts her in the very role she so much condemns in others:

> He hath a garden circummured with brick,
> Whose western side is with a vineyard backed,
> And to that vineyard is a planched gate,
> That makes his opening with this bigger key;
> This other doth command a little door,
> Which from the vineyard to the garden leads—
> There have I made my promise
> Upon the heavy middle of the night
> To call upon him.

The justification for the act is provided by the duke in terms that could be applied equally to Claudio's fornication: since Angelo is Mariana's husband by a 'pre-contract' there is no vice or sin in the arrangement. Nevertheless, Isabella's role in the affair strikes a comic contrast with her own view of Claudio's involvement with Juliet. That the enactment of the role of bawd takes place against a background of persecution and imprisonment of professional bawds adds a further ironic comment.

There remains one further major illustration of the comic treatment of Isabella. In Act V, Scene i, Isabella believes that Angelo has caused her brother to be executed. The duke condemns him to death for the crime, and since the audience knows that Claudio is alive and that Angelo will not have to die, its whole attention may be given to Isabella's attitude to her brother's 'murderer'. Mariana first pleads for her new husband's life, and at her request Isabella joins in the plea. Her reasons for the sparing of Angelo are richly comic:

35

> Most bounteous sir,
> Look, if it please you, on this man condemned,
> As if my brother lived; I partly think
> A due sincerity governed his deeds,
> Till he did look on me. Since it is so,
> Let him not die. My brother had but justice,
> In that he did the thing for which he died:
> For Angelo,
> His act did not o'ertake his bad intent,
> And must be buried but as an intent
> That perished by the way.

Isabella is prepared to forgive Angelo because he has not committed the real crime—the assault on her virtue—but has merely killed her brother, as she believes. This she regards as 'but justice'. She has learned nothing from her own involvement in the activity of the bawd and shares Angelo's view of the heinousness of fornication. Best of all is her recognition of the fatal power of her beauty over Angelo; a 'due sincerity' governed him 'till he did look on me'. What woman would not forgive a man driven to crime by her beauty? The comedy here lies in Isabella's unself-critical, even complacent, offer of her own attractiveness as a ground for forgiveness strong enough to offset the execution, as she believes, of her brother. Christian charity is here made to take a strange form.

The comic treatment of disturbing topics is made possible, as I have suggested, by the *deus ex machina* with his safety net. In this way—that is to say by a comic structure more than usually fortified against the tragic mode—it is possible to contemplate with a smile—at times a very wry smile indeed, but still a smile— a state of affairs which might in another dramatic mode be merely frightening or disgusting. The vulnerability of men to the whims of those who happen to have authority is one of the chief themes of *Measure for Measure*. When Isabella threatens to proclaim Angelo's wickedness to the world he replies:

> Who will believe thee, Isabel?
> My unsoiled name, th' austereness of my life,
> My vouch against you, and my place in the state
> Will so your accusation overweigh,
> That you shall stifle in your own report,
> And smell of calumny . . .

The power of the established and respectable may often be exercised without restraint; in this comedy the fact can be contemplated because the *deus ex machina* is there to set all right. This is however not done until the nightmare of injustice has been lived out to its last stage. When Isabella does accuse Angelo, the duke allows the process foretold by Angelo to be acted out. To Isabella's accusation, the duke replies:

> This is most likely.

When it is pressed, he enacts the probable reaction of a duke who has no access to inside knowledge, condemns Isabella and orders her to jail for slander. The friar and Mariana are threatened with the same fate. We are reminded by the duke himself of what would happen in a world where there was no *deus ex machina* to set things right:

> ... O, poor souls,
> Come you to seek the lamb here of the fox?
> Goodnight to your redress!. Is the duke gone?
> Then is your cause gone too.

A world in which the guilty are the judges is too much like the real world to make its appearance in a comedy without the device of the safety net and the god from the machine. Shakespeare sustains the demonstration of what would happen without the comic protection for long enough to turn the laughter to an ironic contemplation; but then the grimness is dissolved, the guilty Angelo is unmasked; it is only, after all, a comedy. However there is an ironic twist at the end. Lucio is brought to judgement. His crime is 'slandering the Duke', and the duke is judge and jury:

> You sirrah, that knew me for a fool, a coward,
> One of all luxury, an ass, a madman;
> Wherein have I so deserved of you
> That you extol me thus?

Lucio, seeing the plight he is in, begs to be whipped to avoid hanging. The duke's answer is at first implacable:

> Whipt first, sir, and hanged after.

This is an enactment of what would happen in Angelo's world, of what may happen, for that matter, in real life. The duke relents, and the comic geniality is restored, so that we are free to be merely amused by the fate of Lucio and by the duke's serene confidence in his own right of judgement; Lucio's horror at being made to marry a whore is airily dismissed with:

37

In the whole treatment of injustice we are enabled by the comic device of the god from the machine to contemplate ugly truths that we usually dare not admit to be truths of daily life. The magic robe of comedy is put on, and in play we see enacted before us the evil that is latent in men's self-righteousness. The knife is aimed at our vitals, but we know that it is a stage property and that no blood will flow. The 'worst returns to laughter' in a play that carries the comic vision to its farthest limits. In such a play it is useless to seek for moral heroes and heroines; all men and women are tainted with selfishness and folly. The comic vision involves us all, and even Isabella's religious idealism is represented as a limitation of human sympathy. A comedy of this kind is profoundly disturbing, and it is not surprising if many critics have sought to soften its impact, either by sentimentalizing Isabella or by suggesting that Shakespeare was undergoing one of those crises of development that are regularly called in when critics are baffled or disturbed by Shakespeare's work.

As for Isabella's future, we know that she is sought in marriage by the duke, and as this is a comedy, we assume that she will not, in spite of her religious protestations throughout the play, return to her religious vocation but will reconcile herself to the life of the flesh. In the end everybody is forgiven, nobody comes to serious harm, all's well that ends well. This we have been made to foresee from the start, so that we have not taken too solemnly the glimpses of human depravity, dishonesty, cruelty and self-righteousness. To observe these in a realistic play would require an earnestly moral attitude to the events portrayed. In a formal comedy in which, by a fictional device, the persons involved are given a special guarantee of final happiness, we are left free to be amused, to smile grimly at Angelo and to accept with the tolerance we can find in comedy the otherwise tiresomely priggish Isabella.

I suggest then that *Measure for Measure* is indeed a comedy and that we are invited to smile and sometimes even to laugh. In the end it is not only the critical 'placing' of Isabella or of Angelo that we are invited to, or a merely clinical interest in the psychopathology of the situation. These judgements are invited, but they are throughout subordinated to the comic spirit, which invites us not only to smile at Isabella's youthful earnestness and even—more grimly—at Angelo's deep-rooted ignorance of himself, but also to recognize our own youthful errors of moral absolutism as we smile at Isabella, and our own persistent self-ignorance when we critically observe Angelo. All men are to some degree Angelos, for all men have within them both the habit of moral judgement and condemnation and also the universal weaknesses of the flesh which ought to warn them against moral absolutism when judging others. In responding to this comedy as though we are asked to judge others, and not ourselves, we fail in the charity without which the young Isabella and the older Angelo are 'tinkling bells and sounding cymbals' until they are redeemed by the duke's protection and forgiveness and by marriage. When we smile at the events of this play, we do so ruefully, recognizing that Isabella and Angelo are part of ourselves; not gleefully, like cynical Lucios, or with the solemn clinical detachment of the psychologist, or with the stern disapproval of the puritan. *Measure for Measure* is touched throughout with a human charity that may properly be thought of as religious. The theme is a human comedy, but it is a comedy at which we smile in the knowledge that if we were indeed angels we should weep at the arrogance and folly of our habitual moral stance. The very title of the play is a warning to us against the unself-critical judgement of others: 'For with what judgement ye judge, ye shall be judged: and with what measure ye mete, it shall be measured to you again.' This I understand not as the 'moral' of the play, but as an indication, through the title, of the kind of attention we are invited to bring to it.

BEN JONSON AND ALCHEMY

Robertson Davies

In the estimation of the great body of readers, Ben Jonson holds a place rather like a large continent which they are always meaning to explore, though for the present they are content with brief picnics on its shores. The continent itself is so vast, so rocky and steep, so covered with dense undergrowth in which the dreaded Archaism grows wild, where lurking Similes of immense and sinewy length may catch the traveller in their coils and where, rounding a corner, he may find himself looking into the cruel jaws of an Extended Metaphor; the dense fog of Classical Allusion may engulf him at any moment, and there is always the danger of a sudden, volcanic eruption of Irony. So he keeps away, and concurs in the general opinion that this great continent, this land of Ben Jonson, is a wonderful place with a great future before it, but for the present he prefers a more friendly climate.

That is one side of Jonson's popular reputation. But quite often one of his plays is performed by some great classical company, and audiences are delighted by its wit and vigour, its splendid poetry and by the cleansing, purgative effect of its comic spirit. And then people cry: Why is Jonson neglected? How can we be content to remain ignorant of the work of this great comic poet?

Before I speak of *The Alchemist* and of alchemy, I think it well to take some time to speak of Jonson and his reputation, for he is one of those writers whose personal character is inextricably involved with his work. In this he is the exact contrary of Shakespeare, whose friend and contemporary he was. We know little of Shakespeare's personal history and personality: about Jonson we have a large body of fact and contemporary opinion. Jonson was born in 1572, which made him eight years Shakespeare's junior; he outlived Shakespeare by twenty-one years, dying in 1637 in the reign of Charles I. He was sixty-five, but he was already old and broken in body. He seems to have known everybody of note in the literary world, and Francis Bacon the philosopher and statesman, John Seldon the jurist and antiquary, and the poets

Chapman, Beaumont, Fletcher and John Donne were pleased to call him friend—and sometimes enemy; Herrick and Suckling honoured him as their master in verse. In 1616 King James I, who had the Stuart flair for the arts, gave him an appointment and a stipend which permits us to think of him as the first poet laureate, though he never formally received that title. We even have a record of his informal conversation written by the Scottish poet William Drummond of Hawthornden, whom he visited while on a walking tour in 1618. They did not hit it off very well, for Jonson was aggressive, opinionated and a tireless talker, whereas Drummond was reticent and quiet but observant and coolly critical of his obstreperous guest. In fairness it must be said that Jonson did not conceal his opinion that Drummond's verses were less than perfect, and that is something no poet can endure. But Drummond records that Jonson told him that 'Donne, for not keeping of accent, deserved hanging'; that 'Shakespeare wanted art'; that 'next himself, only Fletcher and Chapman could make a masque'; that 'he was better versed, and knew more Greek and Latin, than all the poets in England, and quintessenceth their brains'; that 'Daniel was at jealousies with him'; that 'he beat Marston, and took his pistol from him'; that 'Shakespeare, in a play, brought in a number of men saying they suffered shipwreck in Bohemia, where there is no sea near by some hundred miles'; that 'Sir Philip Sidney was no pleasant man in countenance, his face being spoiled with pimples'; that 'he hath consumed a whole night in lying looking at his great toe, about which he hath seen Tartars and Turks, Romans and Carthaginians, fight in his imagination'; that 'Queen Elizabeth never saw herself, after she became old, in a true glass' and that 'she had a membrana on her which made her incapable of man, though for her delight she tried many'; and—this is Drummond's summing up of this extraordinary man—'He is a great lover and praiser of himself, a contemner and scorner of others; rather given to lose a friend than a jest, jealous of every word and action of those about himself (especially after drink, which is one of the elements in which he liveth). A dissembler of ill parts which reign in him, a bragger of some good that he wanteth; thinketh nothing well but what either he himself, or some of his friends and countrymen, hath said or done. He is passionately kind and angry, careless either to gain or keep; vindictive, but—if he be well answered—at himself.'

What would we give for such a memoir of Shakespeare? Perhaps, on the whole, we are better off without it. But we have it of Jonson, and as we study his work we find all of the man that

William Drummond describes therein, and some other characteristics that Drummond either did not see or could not comprehend
or chose not to mention.

Jonson was, by temperament and education, a classicist and a
very great one. By that I mean that in him classical example was
not a corset within which his imagination was confined, but rather
a splendid inspiration, a climate of feeling and precept in which he
moved as a native and to which he brought his own vigorous life.
Observe, however, that in his own critical writing he speaks of the
ancients as 'guides, not commanders'. He regarded himself as a
follower in a great tradition but not as a man under authority.
When, in his noble tribute to his friend Shakespeare, he wrote of

> The merry Greek, tart Aristophanes,
> Neat Terence, witty Plautus

he surely thought of them as friends—dead in the flesh but glow-
ingly alive in the spirit. This is a temperament hard for us to
comprehend today, when classical learning is so much less common
than it was, but we shall never understand anything of Jonson if
we do not remember that to him Latin and Greek were languages
he read, and probably thought in, as readily as English.

Let us but once grasp this, and some modern criticism of Jonson,
particularly the complaints that he never drew a portrait of a
woman who was not either a whore or a fool, and the complaint
that he has no compassion, seem less important than if we think of
him in modern terms, or even as a rival of Shakespeare. The comedy
of Greece and Rome is no place in which to meet nice people or to
enjoy that modern pleasure of mocking people and then excusing
them, which passes with the uncritical for compassion. Jonson's
idea of comedy was the classical one—that it exposed and scourged
follies. His characters are the folk of Roman comedy—rogues and
the gulls on whom they prey: as for women, the Romans did
not seek to display the highest female qualities on the comic stage,
and in this convention Jonson concurred. He would have been
puzzled by any complaint that his characters are unlikable; he
would have thought himself much at fault if he had made a fool
likable. Fascinating, astounding, transfixing, hilariously funny—
yes, a fool might be all of these; but likable? He would have
thought it bad art and probably immoral to present a fool as
someone who might be admired or even indulged. The consequence is that his plays are extraordinarily stimulating yet
abrasive, their characters funny but repulsive and their plots
abounding in comic incident yet essentially cruel.

Does this seem strange praise? There are other elements that make Jonson's plays rich fare in the theatre. One is the sheer pelting vigour of their invention and movement; the stage is rarely still and we are, so to speak, under bombardment from start to finish. Jonson gives us none of the exquisite slow movements and lyric scenes of Shakespearian comedy; even if he had been capable of them he would have thought them extraneous. The masculine vigour of his plays is one of their great attractions. The other is his magnificent command of language. Jonson writes in cascades of words that drench us and sometimes overcome us, so that we are left gasping like swimmers who have been overthrown by a great wave. There is nothing spare or economical about his style; he never uses one word where seven can be crowded in, and in the rhetorical devices of similitude and metaphor he is one of the greatest masters in English. It is now a commonplace to say that the Elizabethans, having no scenery on their stage, painted in words; if that were so, Jonson slopped about with a whitewash brush in either hand; he heaps one descriptive passage on another until we are blinded and wondering. In this respect he is far from the classical ideal of restraint. He is excessive; he is supererogatory; he is baroque.

A playwright, like a composer of music, must surely be judged on the basis of public performance under favourable circumstances. The qualification is an important one. Jonson did not write for amateurs—probably could not have conceived of amateur actors attempting one of his comedies, though of course as a writer of masques for the court he knew all about amateurs as dancers and figures in allegorical spectacles. But the qualities most apparent in Jonson's work and most necessary in performance—a driving gusto and the uttermost virtuosity in the use of language—are not qualities amateurs can summon up. Acting in Jonson is very hard work and only the most skilled players can bring off one of his comedies without showing fatigue. They require, also, a quality in the player's art that might be called abstraction; not realistic detail, but the essence of a character must be presented, and the pressure must be maintained and indeed increased from beginning to end. This is because each character exhibits a single predominating characteristic which is necessary to the full development of the play, and unless it is kept to the fore the totality of the production suffers. The psychology that Jonson understood and which was regarded in his day as a sufficient explanation of human character, was based upon the theory of humours—those basic elements of the choleric, the phlegmatic, the sanguine and the melancholic which combined and intermingled in a man to establish his essential character. This is of course a rather limited and mechanical theory, but many generations showed the utmost ingenuity in explaining human nature by means of it. One of the qualities in Jonson's craftsmanship that commands our admiration is his ability to be true to this rather limiting conception of human nature, while inventing and animating a wide variety of characters who, without being human in the sense that we use the word of Shakespeare's characters, have the vividness of abstractions, who fall just short of being grotesque. Such drama is taxing to the most technically accomplished actors; amateurs cannot get near it.

What, then, of Jonson on the stage? He was popular in his own day to a degree that made it possible for him to give up working as an actor and live as a theatre poet. His first important play was *Every Man in His Humour,* written in 1598. He wrote a tragedy, *Sejanus,* which is generally agreed to be a failure, though I personally find it excellent reading and wish I could see it on the stage. It would be tedious to name all his plays here, but the most important among them are *Volpone,* a superb comedy of covetousness and revenge, written in 1606; *Epicoene; or the Silent Woman,* very much a humours play which acts better than it reads, in 1609; our play *The Alchemist* in 1610, and a superb panorama of London life, *Bartholomew Fair,* in 1614. He also wrote another tragedy, which did not please, in 1611; it is *Cataline, his Conspiracy.*

What was he doing in the intervals? He was writing masques for the court, and he provided thirty-seven of them between 1603 and 1630; these are charming entertainments, not wholly plays, not wholly ballet or music, but a combination of all these splendidly presented with elaborate scenery, machinery and costume.

He struck a great blow for the dignity of the playwright's art when he published all his works completed at that time in a folio volume in 1616. Nobody until then had thought of plays as worthy of such dignified presentation. We may wonder if, without this example given by Jonson, we would have had the Shakespeare folio of 1623.

One or two more facts will complete the biographical consideration of Jonson. His last years were unfortunate. His popularity waned, and after a paralytic stroke in 1628 his health was greatly impaired. His great patron, King James, had died in 1625, and the new court of Charles I, with its bias in favour of Neo-Platonism and French taste, found Jonson rather old-fashioned.

He lingered until 1637 and was buried in Westminster Abbey. A small stone marks his grave in the left-hand aisle as you enter, and on it is cut, 'O rare Ben Jonson'.

Let us turn now to today's play, *The Alchemist*. I am not going to insult your intelligence by going over the plot; either you have read it, or you have determined to let it come to you by way of performance, which is sometimes a wise and fruitful decision when we encounter a great classic for the first time. It must be enough to say that in the judgement of Coleridge, *The Alchemist* possessed one of the three perfect plots in all literature, the other two being Sophocles' *Oedipus Rex* and Fielding's *Tom Jones*. Jonson was thirty-eight when he wrote it; a mature artist, already in the second part of his life, and the weight and control of maturity are to be felt in every part of the work.

The plot bears the classic stamp. All the action takes place in one spot, which is Lovewit's house and the street outside it. The action is continuous and is encompassed in a single day. The characters also are in the classic tradition, for the most part: they are rogues and the victims of their roguery. Because classic rule did not allow the appearance on the stage of a virgin of good family, the good girl, the reward for virtue, is a widow, Dame Pliant; she lets us know her age very accurately—she is nineteen. In considering Doll Common, matters of virginity and good family do not arise. The range of characters is wide but within the burgess framework: we need not suppose that Sir Epicure Mammon is anyone very distinguished in society; his distinction is in the soaring quality of his imagination. The rest are ordinary enough—a lawyer's clerk, a tobacconist, Surly is a man-about-town, Kastril and his sister Dame Pliant are country-folk, very amusingly placed in the performance we are to see as visitors from Scotland; the language they use certainly suggests a Scots or north of England home. The two Puritans are of different social and educational sphere within their Puritan world; Ananias is a rough fellow, direct of speech and vindictive, whereas his superior, Tribulation Wholesome, is a very smooth person indeed. Within this burgess comedy we encounter, as always in Jonson, a splendid spread of speech habits, trade vocabularies and jargon of every kind, even without including the special jargon of the pretended alchemist, which we shall consider later. *The Alchemist* is a feast of words, ranging from Abel Drugger's shy and ill-composed statements of his ambitions to the splendid roulades and rhodomontados of Sir Epicure Mammon when he dreams aloud of the grandeur that the unlimited wealth of the philosopher's stone will make his.

If I may offer a piece of advice to those of you who have not seen a Jonson play before, do not try to understand all you hear. That is to say, do not rush panting in search of obvious meanings. Much of what you will hear is better understood as music. We in Canada are inclined to be a tin-eared people; the speeches we put up with from our politicians are proof of it. Here is a chance to taste the quality of great language used to give delight and awaken mood and atmosphere, rather than to convey fact or opinion. This is dramatic poetry of a very special high order. It is not to be chewed, but drunk. The players of Jonson's day must have spoken at the gallop, and the players this afternoon follow in that tradition. Do not run behind them; ride with them.

Jonson has held his own on the stage very capably. From the time of the Restoration of King Charles II in 1660 until well into the eighteenth century, his plays ranked as regular favourites at the theatres of Covent Garden and Drury Lane. Jonson's sharp edge, his wit and his cynicism appealed to an age that gave rise to the Restoration comedy in which similar qualities were given a contemporary form. In the eighteenth century Jonson was less popular, especially as the vogue for sentimentalism gained ground. Of course Shakespeare suffered the same fate; we sometimes forget how few of the plays of Shakespeare have held the stage without very long lapses in popularity. But *The Alchemist* never failed to appear on the stage of Drury Lane at least once, and more usually several times each year, from 1747 until 1776—a stretch of twenty-nine years. This was because the role of Abel Drugger was one of David Garrick's greatest comic creations.

In our century *The Alchemist* has had some notable revivals. One was at the Malvern Festival in 1932, when the part of Captain Face was played by Ralph Richardson with a speed and virtuosity that did much to found the fine reputation he has since attained. I had the good luck to see the production, and though I was an undergraduate at the time the preoccupation with the history of the theatre that has possessed me ever since was well developed, and I was anxious to see how Cedric Hardwicke, who was playing Abel Drugger, would do it; how had Garrick made one of his great successes out of such ordinary material, and could Hardwicke follow his example? I had not long to wait to find out. Hardwicke as Drugger came before the curtain to speak the prologue, and he looked so funny that the audience laughed at him before he could open his mouth. He had not made himself absurd; he pulled no faces and stumbled over no imaginary pins; it was simply that he faced the audience with a look of such trusting simplicity and innocence—a look which was an invitation to every dishonest person present to step forward and strip him naked—that he was irresistible. We took him to our hearts and could not get enough of him. He did not push his part into unwarranted prominence; indeed, he made comic capital of being the humblest, most unobtrusive person on the stage. It was a very great performance, and I think this must have been the way Garrick did it. Only a great actor can find his way to the simple heart of one of God's fools. It does not happen every time the play is performed.

In 1941, in the midst of the blitz, the Old Vic performed a very interesting *Alchemist* in London at the New Theatre. The director was Sir Tyrone Guthrie, and he put the play in modern dress and in a partly blitzed house, where Subtle, Face and Doll worked on people unsettled by the rigours of war. Ralph Richardson played Face once again, the late George Relph was Subtle and Abel Drugger was played by Alec Guinness along the Garrick-Hardwicke line of total simplicity. There have been other good recent productions, but these two will suffice to show that the play lives splendidly today for the same reason that it blazed into popularity during the period of the Restoration—it suits the temper of our times, and its abrasive quality calls to something that we particularly understand.

But now we come to a central problem of the play, and I shall ask your indulgence for an extended treatment of it. It is alchemy itself. What was it? Why did people believe in it? How did it work? Did Jonson himself think of alchemy as a valid branch of learning?

What everybody seems to know about alchemy is that it was a pseudo-science that pretended to the knowledge of how to turn base metals into gold. But this is simply not good enough. The expression 'pseudo-science' suggests that the alchemists stood in a false relationship to some true science, and this is not so; they were themselves the most advanced scientists of their day. There was no chemistry in Jonson's time; it may be said to have come into being with the publication in 1661 of Robert Boyle's revolutionary book *The Sceptical Chymist*. But the alchemists were first-rate metallurgists, among other things. And in their belief that base metals could be transformed into gold they were not mistaken; a modern chemist can do it, if you are so foolish as to finance his work. But this transmutation of metals has been the subject of a joke of which the goddess of history is very fond—it can now be done but it is not worth doing, because—so a chemist friend tells me—it would cost about $100,000 to produce an ounce of pure gold by these means, and of course you can buy your gold at $45.89 an ounce.

We are reminded of the search for the North-West Passage, in which so many brave men lost their lives and broke their hearts. It was discovered a few years ago and attracted little attention, because we now fly over that area and do not need it. But the North-West Passage exists, and alchemists were not wrong.

Neither were they rascals, like Subtle in Jonson's play. They had much to offer, as well as the hope of unlimited gold. They possessed a long and marvellous tradition, deriving from two principal sources: alchemy had a very long history in China, where its chief aim was the search for a universal panacea, or elixir of life, which would cure all ills and greatly prolong the days of those who possessed it; its other source was in Egypt, where the search began for the philosopher's stone, which would turn any metal into gold. It reached the western world through the Muslim civilization, to which we owe so much of our early science and mathematics, and the name, alchemy, is a corruption of alchemeia, the Arabian name for the Egyptian art.

The more modern science we know, the odder the basic beliefs of alchemy must appear. One of the foundations of modern chemistry is the belief that matter is indestructible, but alchemy worked on the principle that all matter was one, and if we want to know why I suppose we must say that it was because Aristotle had said so.

All matter, then, was one, and it filled all space, and its various observable forms were the result of an infinity of subtle combinations of the four elements: hot, cold, dry and moist; or fire, air, earth and water. These were not what we would call chemical elements into which any body can be resolved; they were conditions in which universal matter existed. All bodies contain the four elements in some degree, and where they are combined in perfect proportion, perfection is the result.

I spoke earlier of the rather crude psychological system observable in Jonson's plays and referred to in so many of those of the Elizabethan and Jacobean playwrights. In man the four elements took the form of heat, which meant blood or sanguine disposition; cold, which meant phlegm and what we still call a phlegmatic temperament; dry, which related to yellow bile and made for a choleric temper; and moist, associated with black bile, which produced the melancholy nature. If someone was obviously and objectionably excessive in any of these elements, steps might be taken to balance his elements, with results not much more dreadful than modern electric shock treatment. Madmen were diagnosed according to their prevailing disposition. If you make a hobby of

48

astrology you will know that of the twelve signs of the zodiac three are hot, three are watery and mutable, three are earthy and three are fiery, and that these qualities are tempered by planetary influence at the instant of birth. It makes for a complex psychological system that does, in fact, cover all the most readily observable types of human character. A great deal of common horse sense is to be found in these discredited beliefs; their reasoning is absurd, but their conclusions are sometimes dismayingly exact. There is a vast amount of work to be done in these realms of medieval belief which were sometimes so ridiculous and sometimes so penetrating in their insight—just like modern science, in fact.

If you wanted to be a physician in Jonson's day, you would have mastered this psychological system and probably astrology as well. People on the whole seem to have taken it rather lightly, like the revellers in Shakespeare's *Twelfth Night*. 'Does not our life consist of the four elements?' asks Sir Toby Belch, and Sir Andrew Aguecheek replies, 'Faith, so they say; but I think it rather consists of eating and drinking.'

For an alchemist life consisted of complex experiments with imperfect metals, those they recognized being lead, tin, iron, copper, quicksilver and silver; they were imperfect because in them the elements were unbalanced. Only in gold were the elements found in perfect balance. If the elements in the imperfect metals could, by art, be balanced, they would surely become gold. Medieval thinking was adventurously analogical. Gold, in which the elements were balanced, was the perfect metal; that man in whom the elements were balanced, would have perfect health and a perfect character, and might be expected to live forever. This kind of thinking gave rise to the belief in a philosopher's stone and an elixir of life which were in fact one; this supreme substance would transmute imperfect metals into gold and imperfect men into gods, equally. However mad this idea may sound at first a little reflection shows what a daring and splendid hypothesis it is, and how it might draw men of speculative mind, who had no other science to engage them, into devoting a life-time to it.

What these men thought and did is known to us from a large surviving body of alchemical manuscripts and books. Some are in Arabic, some in Greek, a great many are in Latin and there are some in most of the principal languages of Europe. This is to say nothing of the literature in Chinese. In Europe from 1100 onward, at which time knowledge of this realm of speculation began to leak through to us from the Saracens, there lived a succession of remarkable men, by no means shadowy or ill-documented, in whose lives alchemy was the absorbing passion. If you are curious about them, Lynn Thorndike's *History of Magic and Experimental Science from the Twelfth to the Sixteenth Century* is delightful reading, or you may prefer to pick up E. J. Holmyard's excellent Pelican paperback, simply called *Alchemy*. The influence of this new Saracenic science, brought to Europe so long ago, is still felt in a number of English words; when you talk of an alembic, of alkali, of alcohol, of an elixir, of a carboy, of jargon, of a mattress, of naphtha, you are using Arabic words an alchemist would have recognized at once as part of his professional vocabulary. Some of the alchemists were men of the church, like the Dominican Albertus Magnus and his famous pupil Thomas Aquinas. Roger Bacon, the English alchemist, was a Franciscan. This is explicable on the grounds that, while the church taught that the Bible contained all of human knowledge, it was necessary to explore every branch of human knowledge rightly to understand the Bible. Of course some churchmen got into trouble by losing their way in a branch of study that could become a heresy. I shall speak of this later. But if we want to understand the alchemists, even superficially, we must bear in mind the strongly authoritarian cast of medieval speculative thinking. There were general principles, usually derived from Aristotle, which were not open to question; the purpose of all experiment was to support a principle already accepted, not to test it or to derive any new law from it. Aristotle had laid down the principles on which the universe was formed, and his concept of the harmony of the universe was not only highly satisfactory in itself, it was not open to dispute. Alchemical thought proceeded from the Aristotelian principle that 'One is All and All is One,' and its aim was to somehow trap or constellate this universal spirit in a material form—the philosopher's stone which put all power in the hand of its possessor. It was a bold idea, and though science has changed immeasurably in the past three hundred years, and the authority of Aristotle is no more, I wonder sometimes if we have quite done with it. The medieval and Renaissance princes who wanted the philosopher's stone to make them impregnably powerful were not far in spirit from our modern governments who want atomic power for the same purpose. The difference is that our scientists can deliver the goods. Science has advanced at a gallop, but the heart of man has not changed.

There are records of alchemists who delivered the goods, of course. Some of them are very hard to disprove. The account of the Dutch physician Helvetius, who produced some very good

50

gold in 1666, is one such case. Raymond Lully produced some coins of unexceptional quality, made of alchemic gold. T. T. Becher, an early chemist, made small quantities of both gold and silver for the States-General of Holland, in 1673. King Frederick III of Denmark (who reigned 1648–1670) supposedly produced a piece of alchemical gold, assisted by Giuseppe Borri, an Italian. The small piece is now on display, along with other royal treasures, in Rosenborg Castle in Copenhagen. There were others who seem to have been successful, usually working on behalf of princes, but although they produced a lot of gold at one time, there is no record of anybody doing so regularly or on so large a scale as seriously to affect the economy. And of course there were cheats who slipped a coal into their fire in which some gold had been concealed and thus seemed to work a miracle. These were the false alchemists, who traded on human greed, as Subtle does in Jonson's play. But the false alchemists would not have lasted long if there had not been a succession of men of intellectual probity and obvious seriousness of purpose to give them countenance.

Probably the most spectacular alchemist in history was Theophrastus Philippus Aureolus Bombastus von Hohenheim, a Swiss, born in 1493. Discontented with the humble name with which he was born, he usually called himself Paracelsus. He was a physician, metallurgist and alchemist, and what made him extraordinary was that he had a vast contempt for authority; he did not hesitate to say that the great fathers of medicine, Hippocrates and Galen, were idiots; they had prescribed herbal remedies, but he made his of metals, and sometimes they were spectacularly successful.

As an alchemist he was an oddity, for he was not interested in transmuting metals, but in creating medicines from them, and he was in fact the father of medical chemistry, and his uproarious career is influential in the life of every medical student who has to study chemistry, and of every apothecary or pharmacist who prepares medicines.

There was another side to Paracelsus, and it is fitting that we should deal with it now, although we may not linger too long over what is in many respects the most fascinating realm into which even a superficial glance at alchemy must lead. This is the philosophical or spiritual side of alchemy, which gave it phenomenal authority among the ignorant, and also brought upon it suspicion and persecution. It was one of the longest-continued, most thoroughly developed, most cunningly disguised forms of Gnostic heresy.

Gnosticism is the belief that salvation can be achieved by knowledge, and is thus at odds with Christian doctrine that salvation is achieved by faith and faith alone. There were Gnostics long before Christianity, for there have always been people who pin their hopes to initiations, rites, special observances and above all to the acquirement of a body of special knowledge, as a means of achieving enlightenment in this world and salvation in the next. It is easy to see why the church marked it as a heresy; it shuts too many people out. The church says, believe these things, and you will be saved: Gnosticism says, comprehend these mysteries and you will be saved. Thus the two seem to overlap in certain areas, for the basic Christian beliefs are certainly great mysteries. But the church says *believe;* it does not say *understand.* Gnosticism requires understanding; it is a heresy for intellectuals, and not for all intellectuals, at that, for in its highest developments it requires a mystical cast of mind and a degree of psychological insight, and particularly of self-knowledge, that are outside the competence of your run-of-the-mill Ph.D.

You will readily see how the alchemists moved toward Gnosticism. The perfect balance of elements in metals expresses itself in gold: the perfect balance of the elements in mankind expresses itself in a perfection which is to be found in that man whose conscious will and intellect are illuminated with the *lumen naturae,* the light of Nature. He is a man made perfect. And how does his perfection show itself? Does it make him a god? No. Does it give him domination over other men? No. Does it make him a saint? No. But it does make him a man with a well-founded knowledge of himself, and thus far he is god-like, influential and holy. Indeed he may be said to have moved as far as mortal may do toward Christ, for as Christ lived out His destiny with complete knowledge of what He was doing and complete concurrence, so would the Gnostic illuminate.

If you are curious about this aspect of alchemy, you cannot examine it more conveniently than by reading volumes twelve and thirteen in the collected works of Dr Carl Gustav Jung, the celebrated analytical psychologist of Zurich. Dr Jung, who began his career as a pupil of Sigmund Freud, subsequently developed a psychological outlook of his own which it would be wrong to call a system—for it does not aim at completeness or all-inclusiveness in the psychological realm—but which explores the psychological development of mankind historically, as well as in terms of treatment for obvious neurotics. Jung draws heavily on myth, art and literature for evidence of what mankind has felt through the ages about the great concerns of life. It is in art and myth, he says, that we find evidences of what lies below the surface of consciousness, and it is here that we learn what mankind really is, as opposed to what some system, religious or social, says it ought to be. This deep psychic realm, which we all share and draw upon, is not subject to the erosion or the fashions of time, as is conscious thought; though the symbols that arouse these depths of the spirit change from one era to another, the deep contents change so slowly that the passing of centuries is hardly to be noticed.

This unconscious psychic material is something all mankind shares, just as it shares a circulatory system or the five senses. And —now we come to our point—it is by exploring and experiencing this essential psychic material, by means of techniques that mitigate and overcome its essential unconscious nature, that the patients of Jungian psychologists re-examine their lives, understand and conquer their neurotic symptoms and achieve a new balance and direction in their conscious personality.

Do you see any similarity between the Jungian technique and alchemy? If you do not, you need feel no shame, for Dr Jung himself did not become aware of anything of the sort until he was middle-aged and had been a practising psychiatrist for twenty years. And when the idea came to him he resisted it, because it seemed irrational. But irrational ideas can be remarkably persistent, and in the end he had to take heed of this one.

What have the theories of a practical Swiss physician to do with the seemingly incomprehensible rigmarole of the medieval alchemists? Let us put it this way: Dr Jung believes that the human psyche has a natural tendency to seek its own goal of perfection and complete realization independently of outside assistance; man has, however, devised many systems whose purpose is to help and direct the psyche in its great quest; one of these is religion, but there are others.

Alchemy is one of these others. As we study it, we become aware that it has imbedded in it a great deal of classical, pagan thought, the character of which is mystical and philosophical. It is an error to think that no classical learning survived during the Middle Ages; it was well hidden, but it was there, and some of it was in alchemy, and this secret doctrine was part of it. Its principal figure was Hermes, or Mercury; this is why it is often called Hermetic philosophy; he is also called Hermes Trismegistus, because he holds three parts of the wisdom of the whole world. But Hermes is also the World Soul, and his companion figures are Sol = the Sun = Gold, and Luna = the Moon = Silver. The great task

53

of the alchemist— what they refer to repeatedly as 'the Work'— was to divide the *prima materia,* the essential substance from which all is made, into its active principle, the soul, and its passive principle, the body, and then to reunite them in what was called 'the chymical marriage', which would bring about the ritual intercourse of Sol and Luna. From this union would come a child, who would be Hermes transformed, the child of knowledge, the child of philosophy and also, for many of the alchemists who were devout Christians in spite of their dabbling in such pagan knowledge, this child of knowledge would be an allegory of Christ himself—perfected man.

What has this to do with modern analytical psychology? Dr Jung says it is a symbolic representation of what goes on in anyone who undergoes the prolonged self-examination of a deep analysis; his benign and his evil sides are considered, and at last united by him in a new kind of self-fulfilment, a new understanding and command of self, a realization of the best self on the part of the person who, assisted or unassisted, makes this great search and dares this great psychological adventure.

What is heretical about it? I am no theologian, and I do not want to speak foolishly or give offence to anyone here who knows more of these things than I, but very roughly it is this: Christianity makes no terms with evil, which must be crushed and rooted out, whereas the alchemical philosophy and the Jungian psychology seek to incorporate evil, or imperfection, into 'the Work', trusting that when thus incorporated it may be so understood and controlled that it will contribute to a wholeness. In short, we must make friends with the Devil before we can hope to quiet him down. The Devil, who was God's son as much as Christ, must be given his due. You can see that this is not a church idea.

Alchemists, throughout history, had the reputation of being men of austere and scholarly life. Their ragged clothes and their furrowed brows, their long hours of study and their meals of bread and cheese provoked the mirth of people who thought that they were principally engaged in making gold out of base metal. Jonson has an epigram upon them:

> If all you boast of your great art be true
> Sure, willing poverty lives most with you.

But Jonson misses the point. Transmutation of metals was not all the boast of the alchemists; far more important was the transmutation of the soul. But as this was heretical it was not discussed except among the initiated.

To the alchemist his austerity was a condition of his work, which must be approached religiously. In *The Alchemist* we see how Face represents the venal rogue Subtle as 'scrupulous . . . and violent/ 'Gainst the least act of sin'; he tells Epicure Mammon that Subtle is at his prayers, doing his devotions for the success of the Work.

This Work is of a complexity which I do not really understand and therefore cannot hope to explain. It consisted of twelve processes, with splendid names:

1. Calcination	7. Sublimation
2. Congelation	8. Separation
3. Fixation	9. Ceration
4. Solution	10. Fermentation
5. Digestion	11. Multiplication
6. Distillation	12. Projection

The long process might go amiss at any one of these points, and the Work would be spoiled. Very often things did go wrong because the alchemists used such a mass of apparatus, retorts, stills, furnaces, water-baths and the like that it was always bursting— it bursts in *The Alchemist* and you shall see the disastrous result— or else it became overheated, or the heat declined at a critical moment. The alchemists were mad for fire; they could do nothing without loads of coal and cords of wood, of which beechwood was vitally necessary at particular points. Of course they had to have assistants, and you may read in Chaucer, in the prologue to the Canon's Yeoman's Tale, what a life of misery this was; the worst job was tending the alchemical furnace. Chaucer's assistant alchemist tells of one of the occupational hazards:

> Evermore, where that ever they goon,
> Men may hem knowe by smel of brimstoon;
> For al the world, they stinken as a goot;
> Her savour is so rammish and so hoot,
> That, though a man from hem a myle be,
> The savour wol infect him, trusteth me.

He tells also of one of the commonest disappointments of the job:

> Er that the pot be on the fyr y-do
> Of metals with a certein quantitee,
> My lord hem tempreth, and no man but he—

55

Now he is goon, I dar seyn boldely—
For, as men seyn, he can don craftily;
Algate I woot wel he hath swich a name,
And yet full oft he renneth in a blame;
And wite ye how? ful oft it happeth so
The pot to-breketh, and farewel! al is go!

The extraordinary world of fantasy in which the alchemists concealed themselves is finely displayed in the names of their apparatus. Some words were Arabic, such as alembic and carboy; others had extraordinary origins, like the water-bath, still used in kitchens, and still called a bain-marie; but who was this Marie, whose *bain* it was? No less a person than Moses' sister Miriam, who was supposed to have been one of the earliest and greatest alchemists. Think of that, next time you put a custard in a bain-marie. There was also the pelican, which was a vessel for redistilling or, as they called it, cohobation; it looked rather like the Christian symbol of the pelican in its piety—that is the pelican wounding its bosom with its beak in order to feed its young with its own blood. And as there were no accurate measures of temperature, the greatest nicety had to be exercised to distinguish between the heats of a boiling-water bath, or an ash-bath, or the heat provided by a poultice of fresh horse dung. An alchemist's laboratory was an extremely expensive place to equip, and a hot, messy, smelly place to work. The assistants normally wore leather, and the master wore his scholar's robe, burnt, stained and, to an uncomprehending eye, pitiable.

It is the role of faithful assistant that Face takes upon him in *The Alchemist*. He tends the furnace. Mammon says of him:

That's his fire-drake,
His lungs, his Zephyrus, he that puffs his coals
Till he firk nature up, in her own centre.

The rich symbolism of alchemy that reveals itself in the names of the apparatus and the processes is no less extraordinary in alchemic manuscripts; but it is from these that students of the subject, and Dr Jung as much as any, have gained their insight into what the alchemists thought they were doing. I call your attention to the Stratford Festival poster for this year; it has attracted a lot of favourable comment. But what is it? It is a direct copy of an alchemical picture from the Codex Germanicus 598, which is in the Bavarian State Library in Munich. It depicts the Grand Hermetic Androgyne trampling underfoot the four elements of the *prima materia*. To explain further, it is a diagram of the final, desperately hoped-for outcome of the alchemical work. The four elements, as you see, are these strangely linked creatures at the bottom; the rough ones are Earth and Fire, breathing forth vapours, and the two wormlike smooth creatures represent Air and Water. Rising from them is a right-hand, masculine figure in blue and silver armour who is linked, like a Siamese twin, with the left-hand, feminine figure whose brown robe is heightened with gold. The right hand holds a sword about which is a red crown; the left hand holds the Golden Crown that signifies the Great Work of Alchemy.

It is, as you see, a hermaphrodite, a concept of the uttermost alchemical importance, for as I was saying a few minutes ago, the Great Work is achieved by effecting a harmonious union of opposites. Here again you may discern an element that would not have been agreeable to the medieval church—the setting of masculine and feminine at parity. But if you examine this picture with care you will find that the intermingling has been so carefully managed that the masculine side wears the blue colour of the moon and of Jupiter, and the feminine side wears the colour of the sun and of Saturn. The right-hand masculine figure has a green and gold wing—sun colours—and the feminine side has a wing in blue and silver—moon colours. The union and intermingling of opposites is complete.

Let me mention in passing that one of the aims of a Jungian depth analysis is to bring about a recognition of the elements of the opposite sex that exist and exert unsuspected influence in the life of the person analysed. The object is not, of course, to produce an hermaphroditic character, but to produce an understanding and reconciliation of opposites, of which such a picture as this— it is only one of many pictures of the Grand Androgyne—is a symbol. The patients of Jungian analysts are said to dream of hermaphrodites when a particular stage of their treatment has been reached. I know several people who have not undergone such treatment, but who have had such dreams. For, as Dr Jung pointed out, such psychic development may take place without external guidance.

Alchemic symbolism, as you see, is not arbitrary. It is associated with concepts—perhaps we may call them archetypes— that are common to mankind. Very rarely do we visit a midway or a fair at which a half-man half-woman is not to be seen; that it is a fake is unimportant compared to the fact that people want to see it. I do not think their curiosity is merely prurient; I think they respond to an appeal to the ideal of spiritual unity which the alchemists would certainly have recognized, though I do not suppose the minds of a midway crowd are very clear on the subject. So also with the symbolism of gold. Why gold? What makes that particular metal so powerful in its appeal to humanity? It is not the rarest, by any means, but it is unquestionably very beautiful, and therefore a suitable symbol of perfection and that ultimate good toward which mankind strives blunderingly. Alchemy was not for the purpose of making gold, but for the discovery of the secret of perfection, thus putting man on a level with God.

But now we must come back, with a sharp jolt, to Ben Jonson's play. There is no striving for perfection here—only the crudest yearning for wealth and power. Sir Epicure Mammon is the chief striver, and though he is obviously a fool, he thinks that he is fooling Subtle and Face; Subtle is, in his eyes, an unworldly, godly man who can be bilked of his secret in return for the money that supports his alchemical research; Face is an underling to whom he promises an ignominious position as master of his seraglio. The astonishing thing about Sir Epicure is that he is sure everybody likes him. And indeed he has a generous nature; give him the philosopher's stone, and he will make old men young, and will confer riches on all his friends; this patronizing generosity is part of his madness. Sir Epicure's attitude is that of thousands of people who supported the alchemical work.

Look at those other two scoundrels, the elders from Amsterdam, Tribulation Wholesome and his deacon Ananias. They are cheats upon conviction; their congregation has voted that the coining of dollars is lawful, and they mean to get a lot of old metal that belongs to some orphans and start the blessed work. Jonson always hated Puritans, and this satire is bitter. The combination of scrupulosity in the law and coarse cupidity in the spirit is brilliantly managed. One wonders if Jonson knew of Martin Luther's pronouncement in his *Table Talk*:

> The science of alchemy I like very well. I like it not only for the profits it brings in melting metals, in decocting, preparing, extracting and distilling herbs, roots: I like it also for the sake of the allegory and secret signification, which is exceedingly fine, touching the resurrection of the dead at the last day.

Certainly his Puritans know nothing of alchemy except that it looks like a safe swindle.

Did Jonson believe in alchemy? The question is not relevant.

Jonson believed in comedy and he believed in roguery. The purpose of comedy was to sport with human follies; greed and deception were therefore proper themes for his work. He was certainly aware of alchemists as real people, because he was a contemporary of the great Dr John Dee, who was Queen Elizabeth's alchemist and died only two years before this play was written. Poor Dee seems to have been a man of good intentions and high personal character, but he fell in with a rascal called Edward Kelly, who got Dee into a lot of trouble. Dee's relations with the queen were like those of many others who served the Tudors; he first came to her notice by forecasting a favourable day for her coronation, and she seems to have made use of him on a number of occasions although traffic with alchemists was forbidden to her subjects; but at last she gave him a pension of £200 a year and the wardenship of Manchester College. You may still see Dr Dee's crystal ball in the British Museum. Jonson mentions Kelly in his play. But if we seek to know what Jonson really thought about alchemy, we should not neglect a little masque he wrote called *Mercury Vindicated from the Alchemists at Court,* which deals with the subject in a lively but certainly not in a jeering style. Probably, like many other men of his time, Jonson accepted the existence of alchemy as a circumstance of the world about him, knew of its relevance to medicine and speculative thought, and did not think it necessary to come down plainly on either side. Drummond tells us that, 'He can set horoscopes, but trusts not in them,' so he knew something of astrology. We may ask why, if he had no faith in horoscopes, he troubled with them. Perhaps, like a great many people, he thought different things at different times.

We must not erect any tower of theory on his knowledge of the alchemical process and its special vocabulary. There used to be scholars who spent a lot of time insisting that Shakespeare must have been a sailor and a soldier and a lawyer's clerk and a falconer and a variety of other things, because he had such a command of seamanship and military art and law and falconry as revealed in his plays. But this sort of argument is naive. Any writer can mug up enough of the jargon of a special calling to make a good show with it; a few words dropped in here and there and a little common sense work wonders. And Jonson, who was without a rival in mastering the language of the London streets and the cant language of thieves, horse-copers, gipsies and all sorts of special groups, could certainly have made himself acquainted with the process and vocabulary of alchemy in a short time.

Subtle, of course, is not simply an alchemist. We may suppose him to have done the work of bellows-man for an alchemist at some time, but he also finds out lucky days, determines the proper way to face a shop door and decides what sort of sign a tobacconist should have to bring him trade. He is a magician-of-all-work and can arrange assignments with the Fairy Queen for those who have a fancy for her society.

It is not for us to be superior. Hardly a week passes that the newspapers do not record some imposture that is not far off the doings of Subtle, Face and Doll Common. It is now some time ago—during the last year of the Second World War—that the police charged a woman with witchcraft in Montreal; her trick was as old as Nineveh and Tyre. She had, she let it be known, a devil in a bottle, who would tell you if your husband, or sweetheart, or son in the armed services, were faithful, or alive, or whatever you wanted to know. The bottle contained a lump of something in a yellowish liquid, and when the sorceress asked it the appropriate question, it would sink, meaning no, or rise, meaning yes. She was doing a roaring trade at a dollar a question. Since then we have witnessed the remarkable success of the Black Box, in England, which diagnosed disease. There was also a place where you could see a naked and—you were assured—innocent boy of sixteen hanging in an ornamental cage from the ceiling of a richly decorated room; if you paid the requisite stiff fee and watched the boy, he would soon get a bad pain in whatever part of his anatomy corresponded to that of your own which was disordered. How he dealt with certain exclusively female disquiets I was never able to find out. It is not so long ago that an agency in New York was selling an inch of space on the moon at $1.00 an inch. Oh yes; Subtle and Doll and Face are not dead. Nor will they ever die so long as the human heart craves for marvels; while tobacconists want to assure success for their shops and do not fully trust to industry and fair dealing to get it; so long as silly lads want sexual adventures or distinction of person to which nothing in nature entitles them; so long as venal priests seek to have the fruits of sin while preserving the odour of sanctity; so long as vicious egotists want to rule the world with gold. So long, in fact, as men are unredeemed creatures and have not become Grand Hermetic Androgynes, twice-born and purged of folly.

Ben Jonson's theme in *The Alchemist* is folly, and his play is one of the most splendid and joyous celebrations of that undying element in human nature that exists in our literature.

SHAKESPEARE IN WEST AFRICA

Martin Banham

The lecture on this topic to the Stratford Shakespeare Seminar in August 1968 was based around a series of colour slides. These comments attempt to compensate for the loss of the visual material and are, as a consequence, developed rather generally from the notes for the original lecture. This all arises from personal experience—hence the unrepentant use of the first person.

I think I should start by setting the scene—telling you something about the theatrical situation in Nigeria (which is the country with which I am particularly concerned) and how Shakespeare is performed there, and then attempt to summarize my general reactions to *seeing* Shakespeare played in front of West African audiences.

I worked in Nigeria for ten years. During this time I was at the University of Ibadan, which is the oldest and largest university in Nigeria—which incidentally is a nation of approximately fifty million people. During the time I was there, first as a lecturer in English specializing in drama, and then in the School of Drama which we created in 1962, I worked with a distinguished colleague, Geoffrey Axworthy. He is now principal of the Central School of Speech and Drama in London, but his contribution to the development of modern Nigerian theatre can never be over-estimated. I mention his name now because much of what I am going to talk about was the product of his enormous energy and initiative.

At Ibadan in 1956, when we arrived, there was a new university campus and one of its features was a 300-seat theatre called the Arts Theatre. This was of proscenium arch design with a substantial apron and the seating rising in a sharp tier of approximately twenty rows of seats. As our special responsibility was to develop drama studies and theatre activities we were concerned first with filling this attractive theatre with good plays, and to do this it was obviously important to discover what dramatic activity already existed in Nigeria. The answer to this was complicated. There was, of course, a strongly established traditional theatre, especially among the Yoruba, who are the predominant tribe in the west where Ibadan is situated. Dramatic expression, through mime, masquerade, dance and the like is very closely involved in the religious expression, ritual and social life of the people of the country, as it is indeed of all West Africans. There is a richness here which finds its expression in countless theatrical activities of a private and informal nature as well as in the more formalized productions of the actor-managers of the Yoruba theatre scene, people like Hubert Ogunde, whose 'concert-party' has enjoyed long popularity in Lagos and the west; Kola Ogunmola, a brilliant actor who tours with dance dramas in Yoruba based on a variety of moral or comic subjects, with his version of Amos Tutuola's novel *The Palm Wine Drinkard* being his most famous; and Duro Ladipo, whose National Theatre Company specializes in dramas created from Yoruba lore and culture, which are not merely spectacular entertainments but also contribute very greatly to the study and interpretation of the history and myths of the Yoruba people. I don't want to go into this in any great detail at the moment, though it is a fascinating subject for anyone interested in the theatre, taken alongside the growth of a modern Nigerian theatre in the hands of such playwrights as Wole Soyinka and John Pepper Clark.[1]

But to return to my subject, we were also interested to see what the schools offered by way of entertainment and education through the theatre, and we were immediately struck by the popularity of two playwrights—George Bernard Shaw and Shakespeare. Shaw would have accepted the equal billing with no surprise, but we ourselves were surprised, upon questioning our students and colleagues, to discover that the interest in Shakespeare was a genuine enthusiasm and not, as is so often the case in English schools, merely an exercise in 'doing the school play'—and equal torture to players and audience. I say this by way of explanation of why we should have thought of presenting Shakespeare's plays in West Africa at all: surely, one might suggest, this kind of cultural missionizing is out of place, and one should have been concerned to promote Nigerian theatre, not import European drama. But the simple case with Shakespeare seems to be that we have on our hands a playwright to whom the catch-all term

1   I have gone into this material in greater detail in articles contained in *Review of English Literature*, III, no. 2 (April 1962), and *The Journal of Commonwealth Literature*, no. 3 (July 1967) and no. 7 (July 1969).

'universal' really applies. The enthusiasm of the Germans for Shakespeare is well known—they have long maintained that he sounds better in German than he does in English! The Japanese, through the medium of the film, have made their own tribute. To the Nigerian, in our experience, Shakespeare was not obscured behind a daunting shield of school play, education, scholarship, interpretation, academic controversy, first folios, quartos and Francis Bacon—Shakespeare was a playwright who told excellent stories in magnificent language with a brilliant measure of entertainment, excitement and profundity. Quite simply, the experience of Shakespearian production in West Africa renewed for me a respect for Shakespeare's basic craftmanship, for his theatrical skills, for his sheer theatrical 'presence'. I think it is also fair to say, and I hope no one will misinterpret this, that many of the audiences to whom we played were closer to the audiences for whom Shakespeare wrote than one can get into a theatre in Britain today. Our audiences were not the obedient middle-classes, but represented the widest possible educational and social range. One was playing for intellectuals, for merchants and for artisans scarcely literate in English, all at the same time. And the experience of doing this was fascinating, for the range of the audience's response was immense, but *all* of them responded particularly to one thing— the story line, the plot. I think that sometimes this is the last thing that European audiences listen for, perhaps because Lamb's *Tales* and other exercises have rather blunted our ear and fed us with a dangerous feeling of over-familiarity. If we could gain once more the freshness with which the Nigerian audiences listened to the story, then I think that our whole enthusiasm for Shakespeare might be more securely based. Much of Shakespeare's material took on a particularly relevant and contemporary note in this environment. We were in a situation of nation-building, of the discovery and exploration of a language, of real political strife that strained family and tribal loyalties, and it is not hard to play Macbeth's witches in a country where witches remain very real.

Let me now describe the two kinds of Shakespearian productions in which we were primarily involved. We staged our first productions in the Arts Theatre of the university. These included *Measure for Measure* (an excellent story there—the play, Walter Raleigh, I think it was, said that Shakespeare would have written if he had been asked to write a comedy when he felt like writing a tragedy), *King Lear, Coriolanus, The Merchant of Venice* and the *Dream*. These were played authentically, without any kind of adaptation, sometimes, as in the case of *Lear,* with all Nigerian casts, and in the case of the others with very cosmopolitan casts of Nigerians and various expatriates from Europe, Asia and elsewhere. We tried various small experiments, more with Shakespeare himself rather than Shakespeare in any special context, one of them being the construction on the apron of the university theatre—and spilling into the first few rows of seats—of a reasonable replica of an Elizabethan playhouse. This we did for Geoffrey Axworthy's production of *The Merchant of Venice*. In this production we also played some nights with modern stage lighting, and on others we left all the lights full on throughout the performance, which experiment illuminated more than the actors. It made sense of several scenes, particularly the scene when Lorenzo and Jessica are billing and cooing together—'The moon shines bright, on such a night as this . . .'—when the clown, Launcelot Gobbo, comes in to them. Rather along the lines of Peter Shaffer's *Black Comedy*, the humour of Gobbo's apparent confusion in the dark is made quite explicit and a hundred times funnier by the fact that *in fact* and quite obviously so to the audience, he can see all the time. We also had the advantage, in the construction of our sets and costumes, of an abundance of local materials—not only superb cloths, but also bamboo, palm fronds, matting of all descriptions, etc. The markets of Ibadan are the best place in the world that I have yet discovered for finding the complete theatrical wardrobe, for furnishing all properties, from monkey's heads to cauldrons and for providing exciting materials for set construction.

The Arts Theatre productions, plus our experience from school productions—see Caliban doing the highlife[2] and *he* takes on a new dimension!—encouraged us to think more ambitiously, and to explore the possibility of taking plays out of the university, for though our audience there was large and enthusiastic, it was necessarily biased towards the educated and the intellectual. But from this audience, with its generous sprinkling of younger schoolchildren and others, we had a secure knowledge of the enjoyment that we could give wider audiences and the enthusiasm with which we should be received. Digressing for a moment I should add that acting Shakespeare in front of such an audience has various extra thrills for the player. A well-known speech is quite likely to be repeated word for word as you are speaking it by much of the audience. Errors are corrected, points made in argument or discussion approved of, battles and controversies

2 A popular West African dance, not unlike calypso. Caliban 'highlifed' in a production of *The Tempest* at Ibadan Grammar School. We were not alone in experimenting!

entered into whole-heartedly. I remember fearing for the safety of Shylock during one performance of the *Merchant*, for in the trial scene Portia gained the vocal support of the entire audience—mainly schoolchildren on that occasion—and Shylock was literally jeered and hissed off the stage while Portia's triumph was greeted with a great shout of joy! In such circumstances you really discover the lines that are *made* to be addressed to the audience. Suspension of disbelief is a remote problem: generally the audiences were so involved as to be surprised by the fact that it was actually a story and *not* reality! A great joy in language finely used was apparent in our audiences, who literally thrilled to the verbal fireworks and lyrical exploration of Shakespeare's poetry. Again we see a clear parallel with the Elizabethan love of rhetoric—and for much the same reasons.

Axworthy's initial travelling theatre idea started in 1961, five years after we had arrived in Nigeria. It was developed originally as a project of the students' dramatic society, in the functioning of which we were closely involved, and was partly stimulated by the various *cris de coeur* that came back to us from other parts of the federation where ex-students were teaching or working in local or regional government and finding themselves completely out of reach of any theatre, a cruel deprivation after the feasts of Ibadan. They suggested that there would be no difficulty in arranging for a travelling group of players to come into school and community halls to perform, and they formed, of course, an organizational network spread throughout the country which was to be of enormous benefit to us. The first travelling theatre play was an adaptation of Molière's *Fourberies de Scapin* called, in our version, *That Scoundrel Suberu*. Adaptation of material was something in which we had gained experience through the previous years in working on small plays that toured inside the university round the various halls of residence—a kind of act of necessity to keep the drama alive at a time when we were making massive alterations to the Arts Theatre and could not use it. Lady Gregory's play *Spreading the News* was an early and successful example of adaptation in its new guise as *The Gossips of Ewa*. Adaptations to local situations and local idiom, including pidgin, were done mainly by the students themselves, working at first from an improvisation basis, their own skills having been sharpened by an encouragement of student playwriting. Pidgin had two great advantages—first, it is very humorous; second, it is a kind of *lingua franca*—and one disadvantage, namely that we never found we could use it on serious material. In the adaptations, plays would not be turned exclusively into pidgin, but rather pointed by it where appropriate. Some students were particular exponents of pidgin—one of them, Sonni Oti, keeping an audience convulsed, especially in a memorable version of Chekhov's *Jubilee*.

Suberu travelled in a very modest way—packed into an old Peugot 403 station wagon and a Volkswagen bus—but its impact was far from modest. It travelled almost 5,000 miles throughout the then three regions of the federation, heralded by advance publicity of a circus quality, which image grew with us as we expanded. For everyone involved this was a thrilling experience, especially for the student actors who found themselves working in front of constantly changing audiences in a variety of situations —a challenge to which they responded magnificently. At this stage we were working indoors, in packed halls, with every possible viewing space crammed with people. The success of *Suberu* confirmed the travelling theatre as an annual event, and in 1962 we took our first Shakespeare—our version of *The Taming of the Shrew*. Our circus was growing. This time we were one Peugot, one Volkswagen bus and one Landrover. This latter was the technical vehicle which I drove—an experience in itself, for at every bump and every pot-hole on the mainly dust roads, a heap of angle-iron, spotlights and bric-a-brac would hurl itself around. We eventually became experts at tying it all down, though to this day I carry the evidence of one particularly vicious bump and one runaway proscenium arch! The audiences established in the previous year had grown. They greeted old friends on stage, so that last year's Suberu, playing the Stage Manager in the *Shrew* was greeted with cries of 'Su-be-ru!' whenever he appeared on stage. Such is fame. You may ask what a stage manager is doing in the *Shrew*. You might well ask what quite a lot of characters were doing in this particular version, which was well and truly adapted.

I am quite sympathetic to 'treatment' of Shakespeare, provided that one is working with material—such as the *Shrew*—which can clearly take it. This *Shrew* had several modifications. One of them arose from Geoffrey Axworthy's splendid liberal views. How can one, he asked, go into the Moslem north, representing the forces of progress and education, with a play that seems to endorse the subjugation of women? Yet how can you do the *Shrew* without this rather essential part of the plot? The answer, which was allowed by the informal nature of the adaptation, was to have our actress stop before the famous submission speech to all wives and to protest. No, she would not say that! What, such outmoded statements in 1962! What of the equality and dignity of her sex?

66

And so, in order to get the play going again all the men on stage would go on their knees and beg her to continue. Thus mollified and triumphant she sweetly spoke the speech, and honour, play and audience were satisfied! This business was a great hit, but it was accommodated by the setting for the production. We capitalized upon the well-known tendency in Nigeria for things not to arrive, for lorries to break down, for communications to lack urgency, and used the built-in sense of disaster thus created to give the opening of the play a punch, and to win the audience straight over to our side. This is where the Stage Manager came into the picture.

When the audience arrived in the hall they were greeted by the sight of the set booth already erected and in front of it a large hamper. The booth was a simple and effective setting device to accommodate the *Shrew* and, indeed, other Shakespearian plays. It was a very simple structure, approximately twelve feet long by six feet deep, constructed of an angle-iron frame hung with curtains. This allowed for a front entrance, for actors to stand up inside it and appear over the top, and for exits and entrances to or from the back of the booth. This had as much flexibility in terms of the provision of locations and the like as ever proved necessary.

But to return to the *Shrew* on tour. When the show started the Stage Manager entered looking very sorry for himself and announced with great apology that the actors had failed to arrive. This was generally received with considerable dismay and some- times even with demands for money back. Then the Stage Mana- ger, battling against some heckling by this time, would say that he could offer some entertainment, however, as he had the scripts of the play, and if any members of the audience cared to volunteer to read them, then the show could go on. We had, of course, the actors planted in the audience, and they began to volunteer to play the parts, along with many other genuine volunteers who had to be rapidly 'auditioned' and then sent back to their seats with thanks! The Stage Manager then invited the actors to find costumes in the hamper to fit them, at which point they broke into an opening song—a highlife—and the penny dropped. The audience gave a great sigh of relief and a shout of pleasure at having been so cleverly hoodwinked, and the show was off to a great start. *Shrew*, of course, was a play not particularly familiar to the great majority of our audiences on tour. It had not featured on the school syllabi and was not a 'set' play. It is also, of course, a very straightforward and simple play, well suited to adaptation and to the other kinds of advantages that we took with it. The Stage

Manager acted as a kind of link man, talking between the scenes to move the plot along, allowing some of the more basic exposition scenes to be avoided. This also had the added advantage of keeping the 'story-telling' quality of the production well to the fore. The play was produced very broadly—the Stage Manager playing the widow in mock surprise that there were not enough cast to stretch to that part—covering up his beard as he did so with a delicate lace handkerchief. If purist eyebrows are raised at all this I can only say that the result was one of the most effective versions of the *Shrew* that I ever expect to see, with the rude humour thoroughly exploited and the subtler moments given full honour.

The great success of this tour—which ranged from the great cities of the north, situated on the southern edge of the Sahara, like Kano and Zaria, down to the mangrove swamps of the far east, in Calabar—prompted a further venture with Shakespeare in the following year when the production taken was *The Comedy of Errors.*

But it was 1964, the Shakespeare quarter-centenary year, that gave the travelling theatre its great lift. The British Council, wishing to have the Bard honoured in Nigeria, decided to give us the money to do it, rather than bringing out a company from Britain. Together with further very generous help from the Shell Company this enabled us to realize a long dream and to equip the travelling theatre with its own stage. This was a long trailer hauled by a Prime Mover which we could take into stadiums and sports fields, thus opening up the show to much larger audiences. Whereas in the previous years we had worked in front of audiences numbered in hundreds, we could now think in terms of thousands. Indeed this year was to bring us our largest audience of all, 10,000 in Onitsha stadium. As this was strictly a year to honour our poet, we felt that something special was called for, and therefore the decision was taken to build on the trailer a replica Globe Theatre stage. By the ingenuity of Geoffrey Axworthy and of our technical director, Bill Brown—now of Howard University—assisted by Clyde Blakely—now at the University of Maryland, Baltimore County—this great folding Globe Theatre was created, which when packed away turned into a gigantic box painted like Barnum and Bailey's, and the biggest publicity gimmick in years! The programme was called a 'Shakespeare Festival' and consisted of excerpts from a variety of the plays with a linking commentary. Once again this was enormously well received, though sometimes, as our magnificent Calabar driver literally headed off into the bush to find a way over a river where a bridge was down, the company wondered if it would ever get round. By now the 'Theatre on Wheels' reputation was good enough to earn it triumphal receptions, including a band and civic dignitaries at Calabar where Bill Brown, the technical director, had to be hastily presented as Geoffrey Axworthy, since Axworthy had somehow missed the ferry! This, in fact, was the last of the Shakespeare tours. The following year the travelling theatre turned to Nigerian material—a stage adaptation of Nkem Nwankwo's novel *Danda*—and by 1966, sadly, events within the country made travelling more difficult and finally impossible. And so, for the moment, the trailer stands rather forlorn behind the Arts Theatre, waiting happier and saner times.

Working with Shakespeare in West Africa was exceedingly illuminating for all of us who were involved. It takes a remarkable playwright to stand up to the kind of conditions in which we required his plays to work. He has to tolerate tired actors, minimal staging, unsophisticated audiences given to uninhibited interruption and participation. One felt Shakespeare was back on home ground. We tried to be faithful to him.

NOTES ON ACTING MERCUTIO

Leo Ciceri

It is always interesting to consider a role after playing it for a season. Some of the feelings about the role are more defined and some have been altered. It's rather like a child. The rehearsal time is the gestation period and the performances—because only in performance does a part live—the growing up of the part. The production of any play is so complex a marriage of minds—director, author, actors, designers, composer, lighting designer, etc.—and in reviewing a role, so many of these facets bear on the original intentions that it is difficult to see where, for instance, my thoughts stop and the director's, Douglas Campbell, take over. However we both begin with the text. There is no definitive way to play a Shakespearian role. There is perhaps a time when the Zeitgeist will demand the stress of certain qualities in a part, and some actor will, because of his personal make-up as a human, embody these qualities in the particular way to play it for his time: Olivier's Henry V, for instance, or a little farther back in time, Gielgud's Hamlet, and in more recent years Scofield's Don Adriano de Armado, which we were lucky to have at Stratford. This is not to belittle the very fine performances of other actors, for every performance must be judged on its own merits within the context of the play and the production. A Shakespearian text is so rich and so resonant that there are literally infinite ways to play the major roles—every actor his own Hamlet. An actor, working in conjunction with his director, assimilates the text and, with due consideration to the needs of the production, discovers and explores and eventually expresses those areas in the text which resonate with his personal, intellectual, emotional and even metaphysical being. With Shakespeare this last area is often of primary importance.

From January until April 1968, when we began rehearsals, I read and reread the play and then concentrated on just the scenes with Mercutio. The play, for some audiences, deals with the struggle of youth and authority. For me, this is incidental—only Juliet's struggle with her bourgeois father, who is determined to see the consummation of the good match he has made for her, is dealt with in the play. We never see Romeo, alive, with his parents, and both abide by the spiritual authority of Friar Laurence. The play is about hate and the destruction it brings in its wake. Verona is a battleground for the Capulets and the Montagues, and their strife destroys, with the exception of Benvolio, the younger generation. It is not a difficult step to make to consider this idea in the context of our present times. The first scene should make this clear. The fighting between the families should be bloody and desperate.

In considering Mercutio, the first thing that struck me was that the Queen Mab speech was not just the poetic outpourings of a romantic soul trapped in a wining, wenching and battling body, but a cynical and sardonic attack on some of the pretensions and greeds of society. It is rather akin to Jaques' Seven Ages of Man and even runs on the same road at one moment.

MERCUTIO: Sometime she driveth o'er a soldier's neck,
And then dreams he of cutting foreign throats.
Of breaches, ambuscadoes, Spanish blades,
Of healths five fathom deep; and then anon
Drums in his ear, at which he starts and wakes;
And being thus frighted, swears a prayer or two,
And sleeps again.

This is not very far from—

JAQUES: Then a soldier,
Full of strange oaths, and bearded like the pard,
Jealous in honour, sudden and quick in quarrel,
Seeking the bubble reputation
Even in the cannon's mouth.

I always want to put a comma between 'bubble' and 'reputation', and would in production. The second thing that I noticed was the ripe vulgarity of his tongue which produces some of the most explicit descriptions of sexual activity in all of the Shakespearian canon, and as a running mate to this vulgarity there was no love in his life. Friendship he has with Benvolio and Romeo but not love. He takes great delight in physical sexuality but there is no affectivity apparent in the twenty-four hours that we know him. He is wealthy, kin to Escalus and the Count Paris, and has apparently no work to do. There was a fellow-actor where I was working last

71

winter who was also playing Mercutio this summer and we discussed the role. He couldn't understand how the text 'A visor for a visor. What care I/What curious eye doth quote deformities?/ Here are the beetle brows shall blush for me' fitted into the character. 'A visor for a visor' and 'deformities' stuck in my mind.

By that time, we had begun rehearsals here at Stratford. The pressures of the production were then to be considered. Douglas Campbell thought of Mercutio as a retired army officer, older than Romeo; that age, perhaps, because of the difference in age between myself and the Romeo in our production, but also because of the quality of the text. Romeo's text in the first three scenes he has before he meets Juliet suggests the most callow of adolescents, suffering all the pangs of puppy love. His text is impenetrably thick with Petrarchan conceits and heavy with the deceits of the Courts of Love. His parents, naturally, don't understand him, but his friends chide him and attempt to dissuade him from this unreal, soppy behaviour: Benvolio suggests that he open his eyes to other possibilities; Friar Laurence urges him to bury love, probably because he is so young and so obviously inexperienced; and Mercutio offers the blasé and sophisticated advice of a *Playboy* magazine type. I don't think he is trying to shock Romeo— after all, they are all Italian, and late sixteenth-century Italians at that.

This all suggested to me a much more experienced man than either Benvolio or Romeo. These are the exterior characteristics of Mercutio—well some of them. In the text, there is the constant sense of a bubble being pricked. Here is a man with great élan but with a more mature knowledge of the world. In our production he has been through a war and seen the obverse side of the glamour and glory—the destruction, killing, raping and looting. I felt in the sudden change in quality at the end of the Queen Mab speech the suggestion of bitterness and loathing in a man whose love had been raped and murdered in the wash of battle over a town, and this is the root of his disaffection. His heart has been crippled and frozen by his experiences. In the conjuring scene, the sexuality of which dramatically underscores the delicacy of the balcony scene which it precedes, Mercutio's great Rabelasian arias fall suddenly flat into, 'I'll to my truckle-bed;/This field-bed is too cold for me to sleep:' A truckle-bed—no comfortable double bed for romping— but a celibate couch. Mercutio can only touch people with words, and most of his are attacking words.

Mercutio is invited to the ball at the Capulets as Escalus' and Paris' cousin, but dramatically, why? For someone who has so much to say there is not one word of text for him. In our production we found a way of making a statement about his presentiment of death at the hands of Tybalt. His awareness of this destructive man, filled with hate, and his own cold heart are brought together to create the instrument that will put to rest the desperation he carries within himself. We suggest this desperation in the opening of the next scene. To use Freudian terms, he begins depressive and exits manic, the reverse of his usual behaviour. His first line echoes Romeo's 'This is not Romeo, he's some other where,' but there is a casualness, a lack of interest which disappears in the discussion over Tybalt's challenge to Romeo. Tybalt may be a fancy swordsman but he is deadly. If there is no danger in the man, there can be no dramatic excitement in the fight itself. We found a further presentiment of death at the hands of Tybalt in the text which fully turns on his motor, so that by Romeo's entrance he is fully alive again. Romeo enters his old self. Juliet's love for him and his for her have brought him back from 'some other where'. Mercutio delights in the discovery, and the witty Rabelais returns and they exchange a wild set of crude punning street cracks at one another. On comes the nurse whose pretensions to being a lady make her the target for a sharp attack from Mercutio, and she departs in gaiety.

The last scene is full of the challenge to Fate which Mercutio has sensed in Tybalt. Mercutio demands the moment to be 'now', but—it is a brilliant stroke of Shakespeare's to win the audience's sympathy for him—when he does finally engage Tybalt it is to save Romeo's honour. In his last dying speeches, Mercutio repeats three times, 'A plague o' both your houses'. This is Shakespeare's way of restating the message of the play—that hate kills—but seldom does he give lines to a character that are not germane to the part. These words underline for me the whole of Mercutio's attitude to society in the play. Returning from the wars he finds within Verona's society the same set of rules as in war, somewhat more sophisticated perhaps, but still virulent with poison. The contention between the houses has torn up the life of this town as wars disturb countries and continents. He tries to escape in wine, women and song, but like the Henry IV of Pirandello he cannot escape life and in the end, like Henry, brings the tragedy on himself. His awareness is always coming through to him the moment he has exhausted his kinetic energy on a subject or has talked himself into a notion too close to be borne. The scar I wore in our production was a quite possible effect from the wars, but it was only an exterior mark of the great internal disruption of his

73

psyche which he had suffered. His sense of dislocation from the world and from Verona leads him to the pretence of a carefree playboy, when in his heart he is already destroyed by life, and well knows how much of a mask he wears—for me the line 'A visor for a visor' is the keyline of Mercutio.

HAMLET—WORLD PREMIERE

Anthony Burgess

1601 was notable for two great English tragedies—one enacted on
the stage, the other in the realm. Shakespeare was wholly respon-
sible for one of them, in the other he was only marginally involved.
  Mere artists must observe great events, not participate in them.
Yet sometimes the work of art itself will be forced, by the makers
of events, into the arena of action. Early in 1601 this happened with
one of Shakespeare's works, and it was evil, as is any perversion of
art into propaganda. On 6 February which was a Friday, some of
the Earl of Essex's followers came to the Globe playhouse and
requested that *Richard II* be given a special performance the following afternoon. The Lord Chamberlain's Men replied that the play
was now old stuff and unlikely to attract much of an audience.
The Essex men then said they would indemnify the players against
a loss at the box-office; they would pay forty shillings for a performance. They were men of high rank—Lord Mounteagle was
among them—and it was hard to refuse. Burbage and his fellows
were only players.
  And so on the Saturday, prompt at three in the afternoon, the
preludial trumpets sounded and the play began. Essex was not
present, nor apparently was Southampton—Essex's friend and
Shakespeare's former patron—but there were a number of distinguished names in the audience—a lord and many knights,
not all the latter of Essex's making. The significance of the choice
of play would not be lost on the groundlings. The deposition scene
came and went: let it now be noted that once, out of honour and,
as it proved, for the good of the realm, a nobleman deposed a
monarch, a capricious and hysterical tyrant who overtaxed the
people and sent one of England's best men into exile. Finally
came the regrettable necessity of regicide. The play ended. God
save the Queen.
  The uneasy council summoned the Earl of Essex that evening,
but he refused to go: it was not safe to stir abroad, he said, with so
many enemies after him. That night and the following morning

he and his followers made their preparation to seize the city. Another historical precedent than that seen in *Richard II* was now being invoked. The Duke of Guise, seen on the stage in Marlowe's *The Massacre of Paris,* had taken Paris in 1588, helped by a few followers but welcomed by the whole city; he had driven the king out of the capital. Could not Essex, London's favourite, achieve a success as easy?

At ten o'clock on Sunday morning, the Lord Keeper, the Chief Justice, the Earl of Worcester and Sir William Knollys came in the queen's name to Essex House, bidding him refrain from any rash act he might have in mind. There was a huge crowd there, and some cried 'kill them!' Essex made the four notables prisoners, and left them guarded in Essex House as hostages. Then he and his two hundred followers, all young men, rode to the city.

Up Ludgate Hill and all through Cheapside Essex shouted that a plot had been laid against his life: 'For the Queen! For the Queen!' Then a herald proclaimed him a traitor, but Essex believed that the queen knew nothing of his intent: a herald would do anything for two shillings. At the sound of the word traitor, some of his followers left him and mingled with the crowd. The sheriff had promised Essex arms, but the promise was broken. Essex sweated now; he saw that he must make his way back to the fortress of Essex House. But Ludgate Hill had chains across it and an armed force waiting. His men charged, and Sir Charles Blount killed a man, but he was at once taken prisoner. Essex managed to get back to Essex House by way of the river, but here he found that his hostages had been released and the land side of the fortress was under siege. In the evening the Lord Admiral threatened to blow up the house, so Essex, having destroyed all the incriminating documents he could find, gave himself up. The news was imparted to the queen while she was eating her usual solitary dinner. She went on eating, unmoved.

'A senseless ingrate,' she said next day, 'has at least revealed what has long been in his mind.' The city was put under a strong guard and the court now became a fortress. Some adventure-loving apprentices aimed to raise a company of 5,000 to release Essex, but this was romantic nonsense: they had—probably at the Rose—been watching the equivalent of too much television. A more serious plot was conceived by Captain Lea, who resolved to seize the queen and force her to release Essex and his followers. He reached the door of the room where she usually dined and there was seized himself.

A week later, Essex and Southampton were brought to trial.

Essex wore black and was disdainful of his judges: 'I am indifferent how I speed. I owe God a death.' The woman's tailor in *Henry IV*, pressed into service by Falstaff, had spoken similarly: 'I care not; a man can die but once; we owe God a death.' Essex was on a sort of stage, desirous of leaving in men's minds the memory of a good performance. He eloquently washed his own brain of all its treasonable stuff, confessed all and called himself, when he was back in the Tower waiting for execution, 'the greatest, the most vilest, and most unthankful traitor that ever has been in the land.' He asked for a private death, for he did not want the danger of being corrupted at the last by the acclamation of the mob.

On 24 February 1601, Shrove Tuesday, the Lord Chamberlain's Men were summoned to court to perform. We do not know what play they gave: it would have been typical of the queen's defiant humour to ask for *Richard II*. They must have felt uneasy; they had, after all, and for forty pieces of silver, sounded the fanfare for that Sunday revolt. The following morning, Ash Wednesday, Essex was beheaded in the courtyard of the Tower. 'He acknowledged, with thankfulness to God, that he was justly spewed out of the realm.' He was thirty-four—young to us, to his contemporaries too old for ungovernable madness. As for the Earl of Southampton, he languished in the Tower and was still languishing two years later when the queen died. King James released him, and he prospered in the new reign.

The Lord Chamberlain's Men were suspected by the council of having had their part to play in the rebellion: why perform that inflammatory tragedy at that inflammatory time? Augustine Phillips, one of the actors, perhaps the one who had played Richard, gave the company's version of the event on oath. They had been requested to put on a revival of *Richard II* by their betters, lords and knights of the realm; it would have been unseemly to refuse. Their innocence was accepted; no further action would be taken. Still, the art of the drama could no longer be regarded as a mere harmless frippery for the passing of an idle afternoon. Drama, with men like Shakespeare, had learned to touch life in the raw.

Shakespeare wrote nothing for the greater part of that year. Then, in the autumn, he wrote the play which of all plays ever written the world could least do without.

Let us now eschew known facts and enter a world of pure speculation. Let us try to imagine what it was like to witness the first performance of *Hamlet* in the fall of 1601. It is coming up to three in the afternoon, and the Lord Chamberlain's Men are making ready for the world première of what to them must appear to be merely another tragedy—very long, very mature, but, as far as they are concerned, no special landmark in the history of world literature. Dick Burbage, playing the lead as ever (and the biggest and most eloquent lead there has ever been), is in black, like Essex at his trial, and he is busy with paint-brush and delicately-mixed colours on the faces of the two boys who are taking the women's parts. The backstage area is crammed: there are parts for everybody—Jack Heminges, Gus Phillips, Tom Pope, George Bryan, Harry Condell, Will Sly, Dick Cowly, Jack Lowin, Sam Cross, Alex Cook, Sam Gilburne, Robin Armin, Will Ostler, Nat Field, Jack Underwood, Nick Tooley, Willie Ecclestone, Joseph Taylor, two more Robins—Benfield and Gough, Dicky Robinson who is Ben Jonson's favourite, and two more Jacks or Johnnies—Shank and Rice. Rice is really Rhys or Ap Rhys, a Welshman notable for Sir Hugh Evans and Fluellen as well as, earlier, Glendower.

There is also Will Shakespeare, who is making up for the ghost. At thirty-seven he is grey enough; he needs but little art on his receding hair and his beard. He has walked hither from his lodgings in Silver Street, turning his eyes away from the baiting of the bear Sackerson (or is it Harry Hunks?) in Paris Garden: he is growing squeamish about blood, there has been enough blood spilt these last ten years in London. This part of the ghost reminds him how much death he has seen—this year his father, not so many years ago his son. He, a living father, is about to play a dead one. The living son of the play has very nearly the same name as that son who died, Hamnet. How strangely things work out!

He has put much of himself into this tragedy, but he did not choose to write it. Burbage came across that old *Hamlet* of Tom Kyd in the play-trunk and suggested that, since revenge tragedy had become popular again, it might be a good plan to do something sophisticated and modern with the old tale of the Danish prince who feigned madness to encompass revenge of a murdered king and father. Well, the groundlings, by the sound of them, expect a treat on the lines of *The Spanish Tragedy*, which Ben has refurbished for the Admiral's Men. The better sort, in the galleries and on the sides of the stage (tablets at the ready to take down notable lines and maxims), have seen Marston's *Antonio's Revenge*. All have lived through the real-life tragedy of Essex's rise and fall. Hamlet, though, is not an Essex; nor is he, despite the inky cloak, the conventional melancholic. He looks back to a folk-legend, the green man Amloth who acted mad. Used not the Earl of Derby to say: 'I'll play Amloth with thee, lad,' meaning he would be furious?

Denmark is in the news. It seems certain now that the succession will go to James VI of Scotland and that none, since the shock of the Essex rebellion, will oppose it. It will not be long before a Danish queen, with her Danish friends, will be in London. At present the Danes are not much liked—something to do with their poaching on English fishing preserves in the North Sea, something to do with their shocking drinking habits. The man who owns the Dansker beershop—Yaughan, or some such name —drinks till he vomits. Soon it will be vaguely treasonable to dislike the Danes: at present it is in order.

Most of the actors are mouthing their lines; some are taking Dutch, or Danish, courage out of a firkin sent over from Yaughan's, or whatever the name is. There is an unknown man there brought in for walking-on parts. He has the look of a shorthand writer: he will work his piracy from the very stage or wings. He looks foolish. He will have Claudius saying: 'Lights, lights I will to bed,' as though merely tired, not shocked by the revelation of the play within a play. A good device of Tom Kyd's, that. Worth retaining.

Music. Trumpets. The flag flies from the high tower. The play begins. On the tarrass, or gallery, a nervous officer of the watch: there have been nervous officers enough during the Essex troubles. All these Danes have Roman names, Italianate anyway: the groundlings cannot conceive of a tragedy without hot southern blood in it. Francisco, Horatio, Marcellus, Bernardo. It is broad daylight and the autumn sun is warm, but words quickly paint the time of night and the intense northern cold. Eerie talk of a ghost, Horatio sceptical in the modern manner. The ghost appears, Will Shakespeare, the creator of all these words, but himself, as yet, speaking no words.

Reminiscences from Horatio about the recently performed *Julius Caesar,* the portents before the assassination:

> And even the like precurse of fear'd events,
> As harbingers preceding still the fates
> And prologue to the omen coming on,
> Have heaven and earth together demonstrated
> Unto our climature and countrymen.

Denmark is, for the moment, England; the audience still remembers the earthquake of last Christmas. Backstage, Armin does a skilful cock-crow. The ghost glides off. While Horatio and the soldiers finish their scene on the tarrass, the main stage below fills up with the court of Denmark.

Trumpets and drums for Claudius, the boy Gertrude beside him. Every inch a king, he delivers his address from the twin-throned dais. Too long? Well, the audience has Hamlet's sour, sad face to look at, counterpoint to that kingly strength and discretion. Hamlet leans against a downstage pillar, as far away as possible from the upstage king. Now for his first soliloquy: they will see now that he is not one of Ben's melancholics, a black weed of depression lacking roots. The roots are powerful enough: his black is the black of mourning, he is wretched for the death of his father and for a rottenness in the state figured in his own mother's faithlessness and, worse, her incestuous marriage. And now the rage of his invective against the unweeded garden of the world and the frailty of women, its flowers, is balanced by the entrance of the sane scholar Horatio, not easily movable and, in the scene following, the sweet innocence of Ophelia (surely there is nothing of Gertrude in her, but Hamlet will, in his bitterness, see much), and the sententious maxims of Polonius.

Now the tarrass again, and the air biting shrewdly, a nipping and an eager air. Hamlet, censuring the Danes for their drunkenness, is in danger of becoming dull. Good, the attention of the groundlings is wandering, there are some coughs. Now into that dullness the ghost thrusts himself again, and the growing inattention is jolted awake. The ghost beckons Hamlet away, which means that both leave the tarrass and take the stairway quickly, re-entering on the main stage below. The five lines shared by Horatio and Marcellus are just enough to cover their passage. So this great speech of the ghost can be made in the main acting area. The book-holder is ready to prompt, for Will is not always reliable, not even with the lines he has himself written. And now the ghost's morning dissolution: no cock-crow this time, since an effect is diminished by repetition. The gallants from the Inns of Court, on their stools left and right of the stage, are already writing down odd lines on their tablets: they will quote them that evening at supper. Hamlet also has tablets. He takes the gallants aback by himself writing that one may smile, and smile, and be a villain. Horatio and Marcellus have been able to make their way down to the main backstage more slowly—perhaps there was time for a quick swig backstage—and the ghost has had time to get below the stage, into the cellarage. From deep below comes the injunction 'Swear'. Horatio, the sceptic, is filled with wonder. Hamlet tells him there are more things in heaven and earth than are dreamt of in his philosophy. Some of the gallants, despite Hamlet's previous gentle mockery, are busy with their tablets. The ghost, perturbed spirit, is bidden rest. Will can take that literally. His next and last entrance is many scenes off.

Soon we forget the unfolding tragedy, for Rosencrantz and Guildenstern have arrived to tell the prince that the players are coming, and we settle down to a long discussion of the state of the London theatre. Guildenstern and Rosencrantz—these are pawn-brokers' names. Hamlet's two schoolfriends smile and smile and are villains. Curiously, though, Rosencrantz's name seems to prophesy a pathetic death which is none of his concern: Ophelia goes to her watery end with rose garlands; at her funeral she has her 'virgin crants'. But the only hard fate discussed at the moment is that of 'the tragedians of the city'—the Lord Chamberlain's Men, who have come on tour as far as Elsinore in Denmark. Why are they not at home in London? Because the little eyases or young hawks of the children's theatres are taking all the custom. 'Do the boys carry it away?' asks Hamlet. 'Ay, that they do, my lord,' replies Rosencrantz. 'Hercules and his load too.' They all look up a moment at the flag fluttering from the tower of the Globe, which shows this same loaded Hercules.

The players enter, and Hamlet mentions a play that was acted 'not above once'. It 'pleased not the million; 'twas caviare to the general.' The first player delivers a long speech from this play—about the siege of Troy, Priam, Pyrrhus and Hecuba. At once we realize what the play is called— *Troilus and Cressida*. The speech is not in the printed version: it was never 'clapper-clawed' by the mob. But Shakespeare still thinks it a fine piece of work, and he is determined to impose that excised speech on players and public alike. Good work must not be wasted.

When, very soon, we come to Hamlet's 'to be or not to be' soliloquy, there will be some puzzled frowns among the more naive members of the audience. For here is a man wondering whether there is anything after death; 'the undiscovered country, from whose bourn/no traveller returns'—when he has already been given proof, and by his own dead father at that, that heaven and purgatory exist. But the brighter members of the audience will know that this new *Hamlet* is really two plays—the old revenge tragedy of Thomas Kyd, with a real hell to which the avenger can send his slain villain, and a close study of a very con-temporary agnostic mind. Can the two really blend?

And how very piquant is this juxtaposition of suicidal medi-tations, mad invective against all women in the shape of poor

Ophelia, and obsession with the conduct of drama. 'Speak the speech, I pray you', says Hamlet to three of the players, 'as I pronounc'd it to you, trippingly on the tongue', and he goes on to give a most comprehensive lesson on acting technique, ending with an eloquent justification of the expulsion of Kemp from the Lord Chamberlain's Men. Just before the play within the play commences, Polonius tells Hamlet that he 'enacted Julius Caesar; I was kill'd i' the Capitol; Brutus kill'd me.' Gratuitous and irrelevant? Not altogether, for it is likely that the actor who takes Polonius also took Julius Caesar at this very theare, only a few days before. And Brutus, of course, was taken by the man who is now playing Hamlet—Dick Burbage. There is humour here; the two men get outside their present parts for a moment and perhaps bow, smiling, as some members of the audience clap, remembering those other performances. Then, later, comes a very complex irony, for Brutus-Hamlet puts his sword through Polonius-Caesar when he is hiding behind the arras. 'It was a brute part of him to kill so capital a calf there.' What is a joke now will be no joke later.

Later, after Polonius's slaying, the urgency of the action brings in reminiscences of more serious matters than the conduct of the drama. Hamlet becomes Essex. The king says:

> How dangerous is it that this man goes loose!
> Yet must not we put the strong law on him:
> He's lov'd of the distracted multitude,
> Who like not in their judgement but their eyes;
> And where 'tis so, th' offender's scourge is weigh'd,
> But never the offence.

Then, when Hamlet is sent away, it is Laertes, son of the slain Polonius, who becomes Essex. The rabble call him lord and cry: 'Choose we; Laertes shall be king.' And is there not an echo of dead Essex in mad Ophelia's fragment of song: 'For bonny sweet Robin is all my joy'?

With Ophelia's death, Shakespeare homes straight to Warwickshire and his boyhood. Kyd's *Hamlet* play made Ophelia die by falling over a cliff-edge; Shakespeare drowns her amid a profusion of Warwickshire flowers:

> . . . crowflowers, nettles, daisies, and long purples
> That liberal shepherds give a grosser name,
> But our cold maids do dead men's fingers call them.

The 'grosser name' is bulls' pizzles. This periphrastic information about flower-making is so irrelevant here (after all, a queen is telling a distracted young man about his sister's death) that one has to conclude that Will has allowed Warwickshire reminiscences totally to swamp the business in hand. For he is thinking of a girl who lived not a mile from Stratford when he was a boy, and who drowned herself—some said for love—in the Avon. Her name was Kate Hamnet. She merges with Ophelia and his own dead son.

And in the grave-digging scene, before the first clown sends his assistant off for a stoup of liquor from the Dansker beershop kept by Yaughan, the Stratford coroner's argument about Christian burial rights for a suicide are recalled. When Hamlet appears with Horatio, the throwing up of skulls affords opportunity for meditation on three aspects of Shakespeare's career, personified in a dead lord, ('Here's fine revolution, an' we had the trick to see't. Did these bones cost no more the breeding but to play at loggats with them?'), a dead lawyer, (with a firework display of legal knowledge, as though the poet is demonstrating what he learned in the musty office at Stratford) and a great dead clown—Yorick, surely Dick Tarleton, who—if Shakespeare's career really began with the Queen's Men—metaphorically carried the apprentice playwright on his back.

The play moves to its conclusion. Evening is coming on, so that the final scenes can be played with lights, and Hamlet's corpse can be carried off with a cortege of torch-bearers. The corpses that litter the stage come back to life to take their bow. Polonius and his daughter return from the grave to accept their plaudits, and the ghost makes his own shy acknowledgement. The audience knows that this is the author but they do not know his greatness. Some of them would have preferred to see *Hamlet* in its old form. Burbage, very justly, takes the lion's share of the applause. There is a prayer for the queen, and the audience leaves. The days of the bawdy jig—a brief kickshaws after the heavy meat —are over: they went out with Will Kemp. The actors have finished, but they must look over another play for tomorrow— a revival of something, probably a comedy. All this tragedy has taken it out of them.

We can fancifully reconstruct the outward details of an Elizabethan stage performance, using conjecture and guesswork as to what the audience saw. But we have a fair idea of what the audience heard, and it was not what we hear today. Shakespeare's plays *look* the same now, in quarto or folio, as they looked nearly four centuries ago, but English pronunciation has undergone many changes since then, and most of us would be shocked, transported by time-machine back to *Hamlet* at the Globe, to note how *provincial* Shakespeare's English sounded. To give a general impression of its phonetic impact, we have to try to imagine Burbage speaking with an accent that is part-Lancashire, part-New England, part-Dublin. When the play within the play is performed, Hamlet tells Ophelia that it is called the *Mouse-trap* and that this title figures 'tropically'. 'Tropically' was pronounced in the modern American way, almost like 'trapically'. There is a pun there which is lost in the modern Queen's English way of saying it. So also in, 'O that this too, too solid flesh would melt', the 'solid' would sound like a mixture of 'solid', 'sallied' and 'sullied'. The digraph *ea* always carried the value it today carries in *steak* and *great*, so that, as in Dublin English, *raisins* and *reasons* would sound much the same (Falstaff puns on that, talking about reasons being as plentiful as blackberries.) *See* and *sea* were not homophones; *love* and *above* rhymed with *prove* and *move*: the r-sound was always pronounced; a word like *noble* carried a noble round low vowel, not the pinched high diphthong of today. A provincial-sounding language then, but one, as *Hamlet* shows, capable of bearing a limitless burden of cosmopolitan complexity.

Hamlet, as we have always been told, is a play that transcends period and plumbs the complex depths of human nature. But it would not have been written if revenge tragedy had not come back into vogue, if Burbage had not thought that a Kyd revival at the Globe would draw an audience away from the Blackfriars Theatre and capitalize on the Kyd revival across the way at the Rose playhouse, and if Shakespeare himself had not been deeply moved by the political events of the year. It was a time for reassessing, reminiscing and summing up the cloudy nature of things as seen by an ageing man—grey, disillusioned and feeling every one of his thirty-seven years.

SHAKESPEARE AND DANCE

Alan Brissenden

When Juliet comes down from the dance to where Romeo waits for her part in the measure to end they meet, speak and kiss against a background of dance and music. The powerfully metaphysical surroundings of their meeting enhance this supremely important moment; they also provide an ironic contrast to the discord and tragedy which follow. Dance, of course, symbolized the harmony of the cosmos, especially for the neoplatonists. Sir Thomas Elyot wrote in 1531 of the interpreters of Plato who thought that the stars and planets held their course in 'a semblable motion, which they called dancing or saltation.'[1] About sixty years later a provincial Frenchman, calling himself Arbeau, could conclude a book of dance instruction by saying to his pupil, 'Practise these dances diligently and you will become a companion of the planets, who dance of their own nature.'[2] The dance is also indissolubly linked with love, for Love made the world, bringing all its various parts together 'in a well-order'd dance.'[3]

> This wondrous miracle did Love devise,
> For dancing is love's proper exercise.[4]

Since Romeo is unhappy in his love for Rosaline, he'll not go to the Capulet ball to dance. His friends have 'dancing shoes/With nimble soles' (I. iv. 14–15); he is bound to the earth by a 'soul of lead' (I. iv. 15). This punning follows after Benvolio's witty quibble on 'measure',

> . . . let them measure us by what they will,
> We'll measure them a measure and be gone. (I. iv. 9–10)

---

1 Sir Thomas Elyot, *The Book Named the Governor*, London, 1962, p. 73. For a discussion of classical and Renaissance ideas on dance and order see also John C. Meagher, 'The Dance and the Masques of Ben Jonson', *J.W.C.I.*, xxv, 1962, pp. 258–77.
2 'Ce pendant practiquez les dances honnestement, & vous rendez compagnon des planettes qui dancent naturellement.' Thoinot Arbeau [i.e., Jehan Tabourot], *Orchéso-graphie*, Lengres, 1588, p. 104.
3 Sir John Davies, *Orchestra*, ed. E. M. W. Tillyard, London, 1945, stanza 20.
4 Davies, *Orchestra*, stanza 18.

Some distinctions need to be made here about this word 'measure'. Benvolio's final reference has a generalized meaning of almost any dance, and he uses it for the sake of the pun. There is a more specialized meaning to the 'measure' which Beatrice speaks of in *Much Ado About Nothing* as being 'full of state and ancientry' (II. i. 81); this was the name used in England after the later sixteenth century for the dances usually done to pavane music. They could be more or less elaborate and were almost invariably used in masques. On these occasions, especially when performed by men, the figures could have esoteric meaning. In *Romeo and Juliet,* when Benvolio's words are given actual form by the dance in which Juliet takes part, there is probably yet another meaning. 'The measure done, I'll watch her place of stand', says Romeo (I. v. 54). Here the measure is probably part of an Italian *ballo;* this was a dance consisting of several figures in different rhythms.[5] There might be, for instance, a figure for all the dancers, followed by one for the women alone, then one for the men, and one in which groups of two men and one woman would dance together. Such a figure as this last is in fact described by Luigi da Porto in his version of the Romeo and Juliet story, which Shakespeare may have known; here, Juliet dances with Mercutio on one side and Romeo on the other, each taking one of her hands.[6] Shakespeare's Romeo does not dance, but waits for Juliet to finish the figure. She comes to him out of the dance, the symbol of harmony, which probably continues behind them; they are not part of it. As if to reinforce their isolation from the pattern of order, Shakespeare has Juliet identify Romeo to the nurse as he 'that would not dance' (I. v. 136).

The regular movements of the dance also echo visually the perception of beauty and the birth of love. Romeo declares that he ne'er saw true beauty till this night' (I. v. 57); Ficino speaks of love's circular motion and its connection with beauty. The 'divine quality of beauty stirs desire for itself in all things: and that is love. The world that was originally drawn out of God is thus drawn back to God; there is a continual attraction between them . . . moving as it were in a circle.'[7] Shakespeare emphasizes the divine quality of Romeo and Juliet's love by his use of dance as a prelude and background to its revelation, by Romeo's disguise as

5 For this suggestion and for practical help on the dance I am grateful to Miss Belinda Quirie, of London.
6 Luigi da Porto, *Hystoria Nouellamente* . . . , Venice, n.d., sig. [Avi^r]. See also O. H. Moore, *The Legend of Romeo and Juliet,* Columbus, 1950, pp. 131, 138.
7 Ficino, *Sopra l'Amore o Vero Convito di Platone,* Firenze, 1594, p. 23. (Transl. from J. Vyvyan, *Shakespeare and Platonic Beauty,* London, 1961, p. 39.)

a palmer and the wordplay it gives rise to in the sonnet, and by the kisses exchanged by the lovers. Framed as it is in talk of sin, faith and prayer, the kiss here inevitably evokes the idea of a kiss being 'rather a coupling together of the soul, than of the body.'[8]

The background of movement to this whole sequence, from Romeo's first sight of Juliet to their kiss (I. v. 45–112) is a physical expression of that wider scheme of celestial imagery and imagery of light and dark in the play which has been commented upon in the past.[9] It is also intimately connected with love. For Lucian, 'dance came into being contemporaneously with Love',[10] an idea from which Davies made his exquisite *Orchestra*. Lucian continues by speaking of 'the concord of the heavenly spheres, the interlacing of the errant planets with the fixed stars, their rhythmic agreement and timed harmony.' An impression of 'errant planets and fixed stars', 'rhythmic agreement and timed harmony', can be given on the stage by torches held aloft by the men as they dance. Da Porto speaks of 'il ballo del torchio'[11] which was still used to end a banquet when he was writing about 1530. And Shakespeare's direct source, Arthur Brooke, describes how 'with torch in hand a comely knight did fetch [Juliet] forth to dance.'[12] In the play, Juliet *is* dancing with a knight when Romeo says that 'she doth teach the torches to burn bright' (I. v. 48), so it is reasonably safe to conclude that Shakespeare's dancers are in fact meant to hold torches. The movement of these *flambeaux* is a visual presentation of the light which, figuratively, illumines so many great moments in the play. And it is part of the dance in which Romeo and Juliet do not participate together. The pattern of their love is not to be the harmonious regularity of these earthly stars, the torches; and already, at the ball, this harmony is being counterpointed by Tybalt's angry outburst to old Capulet.

The next dancing image in the play is appropriately enough in Mercutio's challenge to Tybalt: 'An thou make minstrels of us, look to hear nothing but discords: here's my fiddlestick: here's that shall make you dance' (III. i. 51–53). The choreography of the swordplay, and its result, is at odds with the harmony of the dance. The scene has other ironic parallels with the ball. In both, Romeo

8 Castiglione, *The Book of the Courtier,* transl. Sir Thomas Hoby, London, 1900, p. 356.
9 See e.g., C. F. E. Spurgeon, *Shakespeare's Imagery,* Cambridge, 1935, pp. 310–16, and M. Mahood, *Shakespeare's Wordplay,* London, 1957, pp. 66–68.
10 Lucian, *The Dance,* transl. A. M. Harmon, London, 1934, (Loeb Classical Library, *Lucian,* V) p. 221.
11 da Porto, *Hystoria Nouellamente . . .*
12 Arthur Brooke, *The Tragicall History of Romeus and Juliet,* ed. P. A. Daniel, London, 1875, l. 246.

is to begin with a bystander, not a participant. At the ball, the measure done, there is a declaration of newborn love; in the street, the fighting finished, there is a death. To Juliet, Romeo kissed 'by the book' (I. v. 114); to Mercutio, Tybalt 'fights by the book of arithmetic' (III. i. 108).

After this first death there are no more images of dancing in the play, and this should not surprise us. The flaring torch, however, linked by Romeo with Juliet's beauty, and a part of the dance itself, occurs briefly as an image in their farewell (III. v. 14), and is physically an essential part of the final scene. At the banquet the torches moved in harmonious concord; in the graveyard, Paris extinguishes his torch as he comes to the Capulet vault; Romeo's lights him to his death, and is placed, unmoving, in the tomb. The stars, no longer surrounding images for love, are inauspicious, and a yoke on Romeo's 'world-wearied flesh' (V. iii. 112). The dislocation of life is reflected in this dramatic use of the torch, which has a direct, ironic, relation with the *ballo* of the first act.

Dance, then, adds to the play's pervading ironic structure. It can also be a physical presentation of a major theme of imagery in the play, and it is a visual comment on the star-crossed universe of the lovers.

In *A Midsummer Night's Dream* Shakespeare uses dance more deliberately to comment on and affect the major pattern of order and disorder in the action. Dancing was a natural part of summer festivals, and while I do not entirely agree with C. L. Barber that the May games of the English countryside were the main inspiration of the *Dream,*[13] it is clear that the spirit of the May game is an essential part of the play's movement.

The quarrel among the fairies results in the foul disturbances in nature that Titania describes in Act II, and she leaves no doubt that Oberon's rude interruption of her dancing with her fairies is a highly important aspect of their dispute:

> And never, since the middle summer's spring,
> Met we on hill, in dale, forest, or mead,
> By paved fountain, or by rushy brook,
> Or in the beached margent of the sea
> To dance our ringlets to the whistling wind,
> But with thy brawls thou hast disturbed our sport.
> Therefore the winds, piping to us in vain,
> As in revenge, have sucked up from the sea

---

13 See C. L. Barber, *Shakespeare's Festive Comedy,* Princeton, 1959, pp. 119–162.

Contagious fogs; which, falling in the land,
Have every pelting river made so proud
That they have overborne their continents.
(II. i. 82–92)

This is the first mention of dance in the play, and it comes after all the characters have been introduced. Hints of disorder and irregularity have already been given earlier in the court, and humorously in the mechanicals' scene, with Bottom wanting to play all the parts and distributing malapropisms freely. These hints are now confirmed, and more can be expected. Oberon has broken the 'ringlets' of the dancing fairies, the ring, the form of perfection; Titania makes him a conditional offer of peace when she says,

> If you will patiently dance in our round,
> And see our moonlight revels, go with us (II. i. 140–141)

but Oberon refuses to join them unless he is given the Indian boy.

The fairies are those most concerned with dancing in the play, which is to be expected; dancing was one of the main occupations of the Elizabethan fairies, and their principal means of getting from one place to another. They do not walk or run. They 'skip' (II. i. 61), they 'hop', they 'gambol' (III. i. 172), they 'trip away' (V. ii. 51). One seventeenth-century commentator, Robert Kirk, remarks irresistibly on their 'paroxisms of antic corybantic jollity.'[14] Flying was used for long distance and speed, and in one place seems to be synonymous with 'trip'; in Act IV when Oberon invites Titania, 'Trip we after night's shade' (IV. i. 102), she replies:

> Come my lord; and in our flight
> Tell me how it came this night
> That I sleeping here was found
> With these mortals on the ground. (IV. i. 105–108)

Such constant lightness of movement is possible because of the fairies' weightlessness; Kirk refers to 'their bodies of congealed air'[15] and Titania wishes to 'purge' Bottom of his 'mortal grossness' so that he shall 'like an airy spirit go' (III. i. 167–168). It was just this effect of airy delicacy that the nineteenth-century romantic ballet tried to achieve when its dancers began using pointed shoes for the first time.

---

14 Robert Kirk, *Secret Commonwealth*, Edinburgh, 1815, p. 8.
15 Kirk, *Secret Commonwealth*, p. 2.

The dancing in *A Midsummer Night's Dream* is almost certainly connected with the unknown occasion the play was written for, probably some wedding in a great Elizabethan house, whose singing boys appeared as the fairies.[16] But, given the circumstances of having available boys who could dance and sing, Shakespeare made dancing an essential part of the plot, a summarizing action and a universal symbol instead of leaving it the merely delectable embellishment it might have been. The roundel and song which lulls Titania asleep in II. ii, for instance, is a charm to keep evil away from the queen; it is, however, no proof against the powers of Oberon.

The clowns are the other group of characters who dance. Their connection with the fairies is obliquely established when Puck leads in the assified Bottom saying, 'I'll follow you, I'll lead you about a round' (III. i. 112). 'Round' here implies a country dance, and Puck's meaning is the same as our phrase, 'to lead someone a dance.' The word 'round' has already been used by Titania in her offer of peace to Oberon, and it is picked up again in yet another sense when Oberon tells Puck how Titania has 'rounded/With coronet of fresh and fragrant flowers' the hairy temples of Bottom (IV. i. 57–58). Again the form of the ring is the centre of Oberon's attention, and here it becomes the reason for upbraiding his queen; this time he is successful, and she gives him the Indian boy he so covets.

Then, Titania awakened and undeceived, Oberon calls for music and says:

> Come my queen, take hands with me,
> And rock the ground whereon these sleepers be.
> Now thou and I are new in amity,
> And will to-morrow midnight solemnly
> Dance in Duke Theseus' house triumphantly,
> And bless it to all fair posterity.   (IV. i. 91–96)

There is no direction given for when they are to dance; it is most likely after the phrase, 'whereon these sleepers be.' A full stop occurs here in all the early editions, and the dance clearly has two purposes. One is to ensure that the lovers and Bottom sleep well and wake refreshed—the dancers will 'rock the ground' as a mother rocks a cradle. The second, wider, meaning is to confirm the reconciliation of Titania and Oberon, and re-establish their domestic harmony. 'In every dance,' wrote Sir Thomas Elyot,

16   See e.g., J. D. Wilson, *Shakespeare's Happy Comedies,* London, 1962, pp. 191–207.

'of a most ancient custom, there danceth together a man and a woman, holding each other by the hand or the arm, which betokeneth concord.'[17] Their dance completed, Oberon can say, with special significance in the first word, 'Now thou and I are new in amity,' and they will therefore be able to carry out the rite of blessing Theseus' house on his wedding night.

It is not only Oberon and Titania who are 'new in amity' of course. The lovers are found 'in gentle concord' (IV. i. 149) and Bottom is soon to be reunited with his mates who had earlier fled from him. The jangling quarrels and jars in the play, however serious for the characters, have been for the audience like the baying of Hippolyta's hounds, 'so musical a discord, such sweet thunder' (IV. i. 124). Of this discord there is now only the verbal and humorous disjointedness of the interlude, *Pyramus and Thisbe*, to come, a sly comment on the earlier wranglings. Theseus sums up the paradox:

> Merry and tragical? tedious and brief?
> That is, hot ice and wondrous strange snow.
> How shall we find the concord of this discord?
>
> (V. i. 58–60)

And to conclude, a bergomask between two of the company, a burlesque of the gentle dance of Titania and Oberon in Act IV.

There is a double strand of humour here. A bergomask was originally a clumsy dance in ridiculous imitation of the movements of the peasants of Bergamo. Shakespeare has his clowns, already inept, performing a dance imitating the inept. It is the same kind of technique he uses in *The Winter's Tale* when Perdita, a princess in reality but unknown to everyone on the stage, dresses up as royalty for the sheep-shearing festival, and then is called by Camillo 'the queen of curds and cream' (IV. iii. 161). Bottom confuses his words as usual and asks if the audience wishes to 'see the epilogue, or to hear a Bergomask dance' (V. i. 360–362); but in truth the dance may well have been heard, for it could have been done with stamping of feet, perhaps accompanied by the 'tongs and the bones' that Bottom had requested from the fairies (IV. i. 33).

Their rustic dance, acrobatic perhaps, earthbound certainly, is the extreme contrast in the play between the mortal and the fairy worlds. It serves as an anti-masque to the masque of fairies which ends both the first night of the wedding festivities and the

17 Elyot, *Governor*, p. 77.

play itself. The words of Oberon and Titania again draw attention to the lightness of the fairies. Oberon tells them to 'hop as light as bird from briar' (V. ii. 24) and Titania commands, 'Hand in hand, with fairy grace,/Will we sing and bless this place' (V. ii. 29–30). This is a return to one of the oldest forms of dance, the carole, a linked dance, for which the music is sung, usually by the dancers themselves.[18] The dance here is first a concluding symbol of the concord that the fairies have brought out of the earlier disharmony. Then, the 'glimmering light' they bring is a hint of starlight, and the stars are a reminder of the heavenly harmony existing in the greater universe, so that in this way their dance widens out in its implications. Third, their grace and ability to bless the palace and the lovers is a binding together of religion and fairy lore. 'Field dew' that can 'consecrate' (V. ii. 45) is just one indication of this. By the time *A Midsummer Night's Dream* was written, religious dancing had long been banished by the church in England; here the fairies take on the function of priests, both Hymeneal and Christian, with power to bless the rooms and their occupants, to sprinkle holy water and to prevent evil in the form of blemishes on mortal beauty, for instance. Their carole finished, they dance through the palace, carrying light and blessings.

In making them benevolent and small, Shakespeare selected two aspects of the fairies of English folklore which were probably dictated by the circumstances of his writing the play—a wedding celebration and the children he could use in the cast. In the same way, the presentation of the witches in *Macbeth* would seem obviously to have been affected by King James's great interest in witchcraft and the supernatural. The word 'witch' occurs only twice in the dialogue of the play, and then only once with reference to one of the weird sisters.[19] There is, indeed, no certainty about their species. They may be fairies, they may be supernatural beings, they may be humans possessed of devils.[20] As the fairies dance at the end of the *Dream* to ensure harmony and bring blessings, the witches dance near the beginning of *Macbeth* to foster deceit and destruction:

> The weird sisters, hand in hand,
> Posters of the sea and land,
> Thus do go about, about:

18 See Melusine Wood, *Some Historical Dances*, London, 1952, pp. 11 ff.
19 'Aroint thee, witch!' I. iii. 7.
20 For examples of diverse views, see W. C. Curry, *Shakespeare's Philosophical Patterns*, Baton Rouge, 1937; H. N. Paul, *The Royal Play of Macbeth*, New York, 1950; and M. D. W. Jeffreys, 'The Weird Sisters in *Macbeth*', *Eng. St. in Africa*, I, 1958, pp. 43–54, 229–35.

Thrice to thine, and thrice to mine,
And thrice again to make up nine.
Peace! the charm's wound up.   (I. iii. 32–37)

Three and nine are odd numbers, with ancient magical and cabbalistic significance, frequently used in ritual dance. Three occurs several times in the play, apart from being the number of the witches themselves. Macbeth's titles are three—Glamis, Cawdor and King. The first murder involves three deaths, Duncan's and the two grooms'. There are three murderers to kill Banquo—curiously enough, in Act III, scene iii. Three apparitions appear in Act IV, scene i, and, not unexpectedly, there are several other uses of three in this scene of magic. The triad, then, is a recurring idea in the play.

One of the more potent triadic images for the Renaissance was formed by the three Graces. With arms entwined, 'dancing an endless round,'[21] they represented, among many ideas, the triple rhythm of generosity—giving, accepting and returning; they were also a symbol of love. Christianized, they represented holy love which is given by God to man, who is thus enraptured and then returned to God in a state of ecstasy.[22] This circular motion has already been noticed in Ficino's idea of love and beauty, with relation to Romeo and Juliet.

As the Graces represent love and beauty, the witches represent and engender hate and ugliness. They may even be the 'spirits/That tend on mortal thoughts' (I. v. 41–42), the 'murdering ministers' (I. v. 49) that Lady Macbeth calls upon; her speech closely follows on her reading of Macbeth's letter which begins, 'They met me in the day of success . . .' (I. v. 1). That they are ugly is obvious from Banquo's mention of 'skinny lips' and 'beards' (I. iii. 45–46) and Macbeth's later greeting to them, 'How now, you secret, black, and midnight hags' (IV. i. 48).

Less obvious is their reversal of the Graces in their character as charities, or thanks, which stems from Seneca's words in De Beneficiis, 'Why walks that knot [i.e. the group of three Graces] in a roundel hand in hand? It is in this respect that a good turn passing orderly from hand to hand, doth nevertheless return to the giver: and the grace of the whole is marred, if it be anywhere broken off: but is most beautiful, if it continue together and keep its course.'[23] An additional later moral was found in the position

21   Davies, Orchestra, stanza 75.
22   See Edgar Wind, Pagan Mysteries in the Renaissance, London, 1958, pp. 31–56.
23   Seneca, De Beneficiis, transl. Arthur Golding, London, 1578, p. 3ᵛ.

of the Graces, one with her back to us, the others facing us, because two benefits are supposed to return for one given, though not everyone agreed with this interpretation.[24] The idea of giving, accepting and returning with increased value is presented in reverse in the first witch's story of the sailor's wife who munched chestnuts. The witch asked for some, was refused, and therefore plans revenge; the result for the sailor's wife will be sorrow, not ecstasy.

This prefigures events in the play, for the circular motion of giving, accepting and returning is again perverted in the relationship of Duncan and Macbeth, as it is presented in the continuation of the same scene. The cycle begins when Ross and Angus enter to say, 'The king hath happily received, Macbeth,/The news of thy success' (I. iii. 89–90), and 'We are sent to give thee from our royal master thanks' (I. iii. 100–101); the thaneship of Cawdor is then bestowed and the triad is complete (I. iii. 105). Macbeth's gift, success in battle, has been received by Duncan, and given back in a more glorious form. The honour, that is the gift which Macbeth receives, should then be transmuted into another, greater benefit to be returned to the giver, the king, and so the continuous movement should go on. Macbeth mars it by murdering Duncan.

The Graces were depicted naked 'because graces must be free of deceit'[25] or, if clothed, then like Botticelli's Graces in the 'Primavera' they wore 'loose garments, howbeit very sheer and thin' as Golding translates it.[26] The witches however are explicitly described by Banquo as 'so wild in their attire' (I. iii. 40) and he later calls upon them 'I' the name of truth' (I. iii. 52) to tell whether they are 'fantastical' or 'outwardly' what they show. They are certainly not free of deceit, since by the equivocal statements made by themselves and by their masters, who appear as apparitions in Act IV, they induce in Macbeth the false security which plays so large a part in his downfall.

The first dance of the witches travesties the ever-circling dance of the Graces and it is undoubtedly Shakespearian. It is a carole, the words being chanted rather than sung. Linking hands the weird sisters make a circle, moving first to the right, then probably to the left, then to the right again; they would certainly have begun on the right foot, and moved widdershins, that is, in an anticlock-

24 Servius, *In Vergilii Aeneidem*, I, 720, quoted by Wind, *Pagan Mysteries in the Renaissance*, p. 33. For a dissident view see N. Comes, *Mythologie*, transl. I. de Montlyard, Lyon, 1607, p. 384.
25 See Wind, *Pagan Mysteries in the Renaissance*, p. 34.
26 Seneca, *De Beneficiis*.

wise direction.[27] All normal dances began with the left foot for reasons, now long lost, of sympathetic magic. It is a ritual dance to make a charm, using mystic numbers, and it is completely justified dramatically.

The other dances, in Act IV, scene i, are almost certainly interpolated. The first is danced around the cauldron at Hecate's command, to enchant the foul ingredients of the pot. This dance is superfluous because the witches have already pronounced their charm 'firm and good' (IV. i. 38) before Hecate arrives. The second is performed to cheer up Macbeth after he has seen the apparitions —a rather thin excuse. Moreover, if the earlier entry of Hecate is spurious, there is a fair case for thinking this second dance is also. One of the witches says, 'I'll charm the air to give a sound/While you perform your antic round' (IV. i. 129–130). If just Shakespeare's witches were on stage, this would leave only two of them to dance the round. Two would be adequate, but the dance would be far more effective if performed by several dancers. Ben Jonson has given a full description of the kind of grotesque movements that would have been made, in his annotations for *The Masque of Queens*.[28] The Folio stage direction for Hecate's entrance earlier in the scene is: 'Enter Hecate and the other witches'. This has been emended variously to: 'Enter Hecate to the other three witches' or simply: 'Enter Hecate.'[29] It is very likely that the 'other witches' of the stage direction were brought in specially to make up the numbers for more spectacular dancing, first around the cauldron and then in the 'antic round'. Neither of these is essential to the play, both are performed to music, which is not used in the dance of the first act, and both of them hold up the action.

These dances, then, are quite unlike any of the other dances discussed in this paper. The ritual dance of Act I, however, is important structurally in the preparation of a charm—it travesties the dance as a symbol of harmony, and whether or not intentionally it is a visual perversion of the dance of the three Graces.

27 As in e.g., 'They danced along the Kirk-yeard . . . and John Fein mussiled [i.e. masked] led the ring . . . The men turned nine times Widder-shines about, and the Women six times.' George Sinclair, *Satans Invisible World Discovered*, Edinburgh, 1685, p. 25. The numbers are multiples of three.
28 'At wch, wth a strange and sodayne Musique, they fell into a *magicall Daunce*, full of praeposterous change, and gesticulation, but most applying to theyr property: who, at theyr meetings, do all thinges contrary to the custome of Men, dauncing, back to back, hip to hip, theyr handes joyn'd, and making theyr *circles* backward to the left hand, wth strange phantastique motions of theyr heads, and bodyes. All wch were excellently imitated by the Maker of the Daunce, Mr. Hierome Herne, whose right it is, here to be name'd.' Ben Jonson, *The Masque of Queens*, 11. 344-53. (*Ben Jonson*, ed. C. H. Herford, P. and E. Simpson, Vol. VII, Oxford, 1947, p. 301.)
29 See *Macbeth*, ed. Kenneth Muir, London, 1962, p. 111.

Shakespeare's use of dance, like his use of song, is always relevant. This is true even of his use of a phrase. When Sir Toby in *Twelfth Night* says to Sir Andrew Aguecheek, 'why dost thou not go to church in a galliard, and come home in a coranto' (I, iii. 119–120), for example, there is much more meaning for us when we know that a coranto is twice as fast as a galliard, which in any case was lively enough. In *The Tempest* the dancers of the wedding masque 'heavily vanish' to 'a strange, hollow, and confused noise' (IV. i.) because Prospero suddenly remembers the 'foul conspiracy/Of the beast Caliban, and his confederates' (IV. i. 139–140). And in *The Winter's Tale* the dance of the satyrs, themselves symbolic of unruly licence, their dance loutish and grotesque, immediately precedes Polixenes' separation of Florizel and Perdita.

Shakespeare does not incorporate dance with dialogue as John Ford does, in its most sophisticated form, in the last scene of *The Broken Heart;* but very often he employs it at a critical point in the action of a play. Florizel tells Perdita:

> . . . when you do dance, I wish you
> A wave o' the sea, that you might ever do
> Nothing but that; move still, still so,
> And own no other function.   (IV. iii. 140–143)

The phrase 'move still, still so' perfectly contains the idea of movement which remains nevertheless in one place; a wave rising and slipping back, a dancer swaying to and fro, back and forth; a ring of dancers moving in a round, circling the 'still point of the turning world.' So often the dances in Shakespeare are at a point in the play on which the action turns. The meeting of Romeo and Juliet, the reconciliation of Oberon and Titania, and the moment before Macbeth meets the witches for the first time are three of these. And, almost always, Shakespeare's dances are a physical representation of the great theme of order and harmony in man as part of the universe.

MEASURE FOR MEASURE

J. A. Lavin

There is probably more misinformation circulated about Shakespeare and his plays than about any other author or body of literature. For instance, in a newspaper review of the 1969 Stratford (Ontario) production of *Measure for Measure,* somebody writing under the name of Korky Koroluk makes two assertions about the play:

> *Measure for Measure* (he or she writes) is not as well known as many of Shakespeare's plays. It was a critical disaster in its earlier performances, and though performed more often now, is still not popular with repertory companies and remains little known to the public at large.

Further, we are told,

> . . . the first act lagged, wandering without direction. But this is a criticism that has been common since the play was written.

Now the fact of the matter is, that there is not a shred of evidence to support the assertion that *Measure for Measure* was 'a critical disaster in its earlier performances', about which we happen to know absolutely nothing. And as for the second assertion, it is necessary to point out that the reviewer has made the elementary mistake of talking about the way in which the first act was performed in this particular production, and the way in which Shakespeare wrote it, as though they were the same thing. Apart from this confusion it is simply not true that the first act of *Measure for Measure* has been criticized for its faulty construction 'since the play was written.'

The first we hear of *Measure for Measure* is in 1604, when it is recorded that a play of that name by 'Shaxberd' was performed before King James I on 26 December. Various allusions in the dialogue suggest that the play had been written and performed during the preceding summer. But no further references to it, or performances of it, are recorded until 1662, apart from its appearance in the four folios and one or two quotations from it which were included in a poetry anthology in 1655. So we can't possibly say that 'it was a critical disaster in its earlier performances', or that criticism of the first act's structure 'has been common since the play was written.'

It is true, however, that the discontinuous history of this comedy on the stage probably indicates that it has not been popular with playgoers until this century or, at least, not as popular as some of Shakespeare's other plays. During the 1660s it suffered the common mistreatment of adaptation to suit Restoration theatrical fashions when Sir William Davenant combined its plot with that of *Much Ado about Nothing,* and called the resulting travesty *The Law Against Lovers.* In it he made Benedick Angelo's brother, married off Isabella to Angelo, and invented for Beatrice a very young sister, Viola, who sings several songs. Mariana and the bed trick disappear, and in the last act Benedick leads a rebel army against Angelo and attacks the prison in which Claudio and Juliet are kept. Pepys records in his *Diary* that he saw this travesty on 18 February 1662, and that he thought it 'a good play, and well performed, especially the little girl's dancing and singing.' Davenant's adaptation is said to have had a temporary success.

But it was not until 1672, when John Dryden published his *Conquest of Granada,* that the first critical comment about the play got into print. Dryden, of course, was chiefly interested in demonstrating the superiority of the Restoration dramatists over what he regarded as their crude Elizabethan and Jacobean predecessors, who had ignored the classical unities for, as he says, 'the times were ignorant in which they lived', and he continues,

> Poetry was then, if not in its infancy among us, at least not arrived to its vigour and maturity: witness the lameness of their plots: many of which, especially those which they writ first (for even that age refined itself in some measure) were made up of some ridiculous, incoherent story, which in one play many times took up the business of an age. I suppose I need not name *Pericles, Prince of Tyre,* nor the historical plays of Shakespeare, besides many of the rest, as the *Winter's Tale, Love's Labour Lost, Measure for Measure,* which were either grounded on impossibilities, or at least, so meanly written, that the Comedy neither caused your mirth, nor the serious part your concernment.

Twenty years later, in quite rightly pointing out that Dryden had imported most of his classical critical ideas from France, Gerard

Langbaine defended 'Honest Shakespeare', whom he reminds us was 'as much a Stranger to French as Latin', and remarks rather tartly that '*Measure for Measure,* however despised by Mr Dryden, with his *Much Ado about Nothing* were believed by Sir William Davenant to have Wit enough in them to make one good play'— an unfortunately back-handed compliment.

After suffering another adaptation by Charles Gildon at the turn of the century, *Measure for Measure* was revived in 1720, was often performed during the time of Garrick and was also given by Kemble with Mrs Siddons playing the part of Isabella. In the nineteenth century interest in the play suffered a relapse: the Victorians could hardly be expected to relish either its probing of sexual mores or its questioning of the nature of authority. Nevertheless it did receive one production by Samuel Phelps at Sadler's Wells.

In the present century *Measure for Measure* has come back into the Shakespearian repertory, as have many of his other plays which suffered eclipses during the eighteenth and nineteenth centuries, often because they were at that time known only in debased versions. Oscar Asche produced it in London at the Adelphi in 1906, when for one performance the famous actress Ellen Terry celebrated her fiftieth year on the stage by playing the part of Francisca the nun, who has only nine lines. Two years later William Poel, who pioneered productions of Shakespeare which attempted to get away from the baroque lushness and archaeological splendours of Victorian stage settings, did a *Measure for Measure* at Manchester and Stratford-on-Avon. Manchester was puzzled by Poel's attempt to give the visual effect of an Elizabethan stage within the picture-frame of a modern proscenium arch, but at Stratford a number of townspeople, led by the vicar, asserted that the play was unfit for public performance. This, even though Poel had cut and manipulated the text, had got through the play without using the word 'bawd', and had even substituted the word 'self' for 'body' in the line, 'By yielding up thy body to my will.' As the plays *Hair, Che* and *Futz* testify, or as one can quickly ascertain here in Stratford by going to see the productions of *Occasional Seasoning* at the Canadian Place Theatre, or of *The Satyricon* at the Avon Theatre, public tastes have indeed changed since 1908.

There were two or three English productions of *Measure for Measure* in the 1920s, before Tyrone Guthrie directed it on a permanent set at the Old Vic in 1933. In this production Charles Laughton played a surprisingly frightening Angelo, pacing the stage tormentedly in a black watered-silk robe and spitting out his speeches at Isabella, played by Flora Robson whose performance, according to Guthrie, reminded one of 'an uncompromising and splendid young Scotswoman in difficulties on the Continent.' Six years later Guthrie directed another *Measure for Measure*, this time with Emlyn Williams as a pale, rigid Angelo, 'charged and sibilant in a blond wig.' John Gielgud also played the role, at Stratford-on-Avon in 1950, and *Measure for Measure* was the play which was performed on the very last night of the Old Vic in 1963, when that organization ceased to exist.

This brief stage-history of the play is intended to show that it has not been universally unpopular, and that in England some of the best-known actors and directors have considered it worth their attention. At Stratford-on-Avon in particular, four separate productions of it were staged between 1945 and 1960, while in the same period *Twelfth Night, Macbeth* and *The Taming of the Shrew* were also given four productions, though one tends to think of those plays as much more popular. Professor Sanders was therefore perhaps right when in 1963 he speculated that *Measure for Measure* was coming into public favour because its 'mood of dark questioning and atmosphere of bitterness (as long defined by academic critics) are felt instinctively to be in tune with the disturbed conditions of our times' (*Shakespeare Survey*, 16 [1963], 22). Furthermore, it should be noted that my examples have been limited to British productions, and have not taken into account the number of times the play may have been put on recently at such places as the Shakespeare festivals of Connecticut, San Diego, Ashland, Antioch, Phoenix, New York, Boulder (Colorado) or in Europe and Russia. It should also be remembered that in Britain alone at least fifty different amateur and professional productions of various Shakespeare plays have been mounted in every year since 1946. The few professional productions of *Measure for Measure* that I mentioned probably represent only a fraction of the total number of productions that the play has been given in this century.

But if the theatrical fortunes of *Measure for Measure* have been uncertain until fairly recently, its critical reception has been even more mixed. Dryden, as we saw, at the end of the seventeenth century dismissed the play for being 'grounded on impossibilities' and 'meanly written', and though Dr Johnson stated that the play revealed Shakespeare's 'knowledge of human nature', it was a long time before anyone else would grant even that. At the beginning of the nineteenth century Coleridge, for instance, whose comments on other Shakespearian plays are so valuable, labelled this one 'painful', 'disgusting' and 'horrible', while for the Victorians the play's main interest, or perhaps one should say virtue, was to be found in Isabella's chastity. In keeping with the critical habit of the day the Victorians endowed her with biographical reality, rhapsodized over her virginity, and praised her as 'stainless', 'incorruptible' and 'adorable'. But the unanimity of opinion about Isabella which was shared by the virginophiles did not last long, and in the present century, as Ernest Schanzer has said, no other play of Shakespeare has given rise to 'such violent, eccentric and mutually opposed responses.'

The play was included among the Comedies in the *First Folio*, but there has been considerable disagreement even about how the play should be categorized. And if it is accepted as a comedy, what kind of comedy is it? Coleridge had argued that our sense of justice is revolted by the pardon of Angelo who is guilty, at least in intent, of both rape and murder; that Claudio is weak; that Isabella is an unamiable and unsatisfactory heroine who thinks her chastity more valuable than her brother's life, and that the so-called happy ending of the play is unconvincing because it is unearned. The late nineteenth century offered the explanation that this dark and cynical comedy stemmed from some personal tragedy in Shakespeare's own life. Edward Dowden, in his book *Shakespeare: A Critical Study of His Mind and Art,* gave his chapters titles such as 'On the Heights' and 'In the Depths', and treated the plays as documents from which Shakespeare's spiritual biography could be deciphered. While this might seem at first glance to have some validity in the case of *Measure for Measure,* which was written at about the same time as the great tragedies *Othello, King Lear* and *Macbeth,* it ignores the fact that we don't know whether *A Midsummer Night's Dream* or *Romeo and Juliet* came first, although they both belong to the same period of Shakespeare's career, and that later Shakespeare wrote plays as different as *The Merry Wives of Windsor, Twelfth Night* and *Hamlet* all at about the same time.

While it is now generally agreed that the personal sorrows of Shakespeare and a general turn-of-the-century gloom are both mythical, there is no agreement among the critics about any other aspect of *Measure for Measure.* What kind of a comedy is it—romantic, satiric, Jonsonian or exemplary? And what is it actually about—is it a revelation of Christian doctrine, as some critics claim, a parable primarily concerned with fall and redemption, sin, remorse, grace and forgiveness; or is it non-theological, focussing on the general moral problems of mercy and justice, hypocrisy, seeming and reality, the inequity of the law? And depending on the answers to these questions are others: is Shakespeare in this play more interested in his themes than in his characters? Are the characters meant to be believable, to be accepted as naturalistic, or are they mainly vehicles for ideas, moral exempla within an allegorical framework?

That such questions can be asked about *Measure for Measure* explains why it is usually placed among Shakespeare's so-called 'dark' or 'problem' Comedies, and why there have been at least three books devoted solely to a study of this particular play. If the quantity of critical disagreement is anything to go by it is apparent that *Measure for Measure* is anything but a simple play, that its ambiguities have made possible a variety of interpretations and that therefore any simplistic or schematic account of it is likely to be wrong.

It would be very easy to provide an utterly misleading view of the play, not by inventing for it features that do not exist, but simply by stressing the importance of some facets and ignoring others. Merely providing an analysis of individual characters, or listing the play's themes, or investigating separately its structure, meaning and style, will not suffice if the play is to be seen as a whole. The analysis of a single character, for instance, often overlooks the fact that in production such a character is seen in context; that our response to him is conditioned not only by what he says or does himself, but also by how other characters treat him. Our view of Duke Vincentio's manipulative skills is affected by seeing that his successful arrangement of the bed trick for Mariana and Angelo will not necessarily save Claudio's life, and we smile at his surprise when he makes this discovery himself. And our view of Angelo's administration of justice is necessarily coloured by the contrast provided by Escalus, whose whole attitude constantly reminds us that an alternative and preferable method is available. Indeed, in Escalus's interrogation of Elbow, Froth and Pompey we have a demonstration of the fact that his more tolerant and therefore better-natured investigation is much likelier to uncover the relevant facts than is Angelo's impatient harshness.

Similarly, if we are to understand Isabella we must examine not only what she says and does, but also her function in the plot and her relationship to other characters. We might begin by asking why Shakespeare makes her so different from Cassandra, the corresponding female character in his chief source, George Whetstone's two-part play *Promos and Cassandra,* which was published in 1578. Whetstone made a prose version of the story for his collection of tales, *The Heptameron of Civil Discourses* (1582), and Shakespeare also seems to have known Whetstone's Italian source, Geraldi Cinthio's *Hecatomithi* (1565) and Cinthio's dramatized version of the story.

Shakespeare made some important changes in the plot as he found it in Whetstone's play, though he retained the basic situation. In Whetstone Cassandra pleads with Promos for the life of her brother Andrugio, who has been condemned to death for fornication. Promos promises a pardon in return for intercourse with Cassandra, who first refuses but later consents after her brother begs to be saved. Promos takes her virginity but then breaks his bargain and orders the jailer to decapitate Andrugio and present the head to Cassandra. Instead, the sympathetic jailer conceals Andrugio and gives Cassandra the head of a recently executed criminal. Its reception drives her to thoughts of suicide, but she first appeals to the king and seeks vengeance on Promos. The king upholds her complaint and orders that Promos marry her and then immediately be put to death. Once married, Cassandra does a *volte face* and pleads to the king for her new husband's life. Although the king has no intention of commuting the sentence, Promos is finally spared and pardoned when the brother, who has been living in disguise, hears of Cassandra's predicament, reveals himself to the king, and brings about the play's happy ending.

The changes Shakespeare made to this story are interesting. He first of all removed some of the most obviously unsatisfactory details. In Whetstone's version the fact that the heroine has to submit to the villain's proposition, and is afterwards married to him by royal command, outrages our sensibilities. Though Promos uses blackmail rather than physical force to achieve his sexual goal, he is morally guilty of rape, and to compel Cassandra to marry her rapist is to add insult to the original injury. Once married, her abrupt change of attitude, from hatred to love, is simply not credible, and Shakespeare apparently felt so too, for in *Measure for Measure* Isabella does not yield to Angelo; her place is taken instead by Mariana. Since Mariana is in love with Angelo, she does not object either to substituting for Isabella in the bed trick, or to being married to Angelo afterwards. Shakespeare is thus able to make credible that part of the story's last scene in which the wronged girl pleads for her violater's life. In *Measure for Measure* Isabella, prompted by Mariana, does plead for Angelo's life, but since she has not been violated and since, through the use of the bed trick, Angelo's earlier contract to the faithful Mariana has been consummated, her plea appears much more credible than does Cassandra's. And since she still thinks that Angelo is guilty of her brother's death her behaviour takes on the force of a moral exemplum: she is demonstrating Christian charity in action, and by returning good for evil rather than demanding an eye for an eye she is illustrating one of the various meanings of Shakespeare's title.

The phrase *Measure for Measure* is ultimately traceable to the Sermon on the Mount: 'Judge not, that ye be not judged. For with what measure ye mete, it shall be measured to you again', and Isabella is made by Shakespeare to refer explicitly to the New Testament emphasis on mercy as opposed to the Old Testament emphasis on revenge as justice when she reminds the Duke and the audience that all men are pardoned sinners, and therefore must forgive:

> Why, all the souls that were, were forfeit once;
> And he that might the vantage best have took
> Found out the remedy.   (II. ii. 73–75)

Six or seven years before writing *Measure for Measure* Shakespeare had already grappled with the paradox of mercy and justice in *The Merchant of Venice,* and had successfully dramatized some of the complexities of the problem by creating the most famous trial scene in all drama. It may have been his interest in this intellectual and moral problem that led him to seize upon the unpromising material of *Promos and Cassandra* and transform it into an infinitely more sophisticated play. What this transformation entailed, quite apart from matters of plot and characterization, may be illustrated by comparing Shakespeare's flexible blank verse with Whetstone's monotonous doggerel. Here, in Whetstone's play, is Cassandra bewailing her brother's arrest:

> The law is so severe in scourging fleshly sin,
> As marriage to work after-mends doth seldom favour win—
> A law first made of zeal, but wrested much amiss.
> Faults should be measured by desert, but all is one in this:
> A lecher fired with lust is punished nor more
> Than he which fell through force of love, whose
> marriage salves his sore;
> So that poor I despair of my Andrugio's life.
> O would my days might end with his, for to appease my
> strife.

Whetstone's play, of course, gave Shakespeare his basic situation and theme, which may be regarded in structural terms either as a triangle involving Angelo, Isabella and Claudio, or as two pairs, each of which we are made to see in contrast to the other. Thus, to state the obvious, we see the lust of Angelo for Isabella not merely in its own terms but also in the light of the sexual activities of Claudio and Juliet, with whose affectionate love it is made to contrast. But the structural units of the play overlap, for with Shakespeare's addition of Mariana to Whetstone's plot, the Angelo-Isabella pairing becomes a triangle. Moreover, the true love of Claudio and Juliet is not only made to contrast with Angelo's lust for Isabella and desertion of Mariana, but the latter situation is further counterpointed in the sub-plot by Lucio's desertion of Kate Keepdown. In addition, the bearing of Lucio's illegitimate child by Kate provides a parallel which has the inevitable effect of calling into question our initially romantic or sentimental response to Juliet's pregnancy. These various relationships are deliberately manipulated by Shakespeare to contrive a contrapuntal effect, through which we are made to see the uncertainty of moral absolutes.

But, as different critics have shown, *Measure for Measure* makes use of several other plot elements in addition to the central situation provided by Whetstone, and Shakespeare has combined these to enrich the multifarious implications of the play. Angelo's story may be categorized as that of the 'Corrupt Magistrate', of which there are many analogues; in folklore this motif is usually identified as the 'Monstrous Ransom'. The encounters of the Duke and Lucio may similarly be recognized as belonging to the legend of the 'Disguised Ruler', and the events involving Mariana as deriving from the story of the 'Substituted Bedmate'. Furthermore, both Mariana and Isabella herself belong to the long line of virtuous heroines who make their appearance in one or another version of the 'Patient Griselda' story, a theme probably even better known in folklore and literature than those just mentioned, and Isabella's predicament also parallels that of the heroine in the story of Susanna and the Elders, where sexual blackmail is also the central motif.

The survival of these stories and their wide distribution is a comment on their continued appeal for audiences everywhere; this continued appeal suggests that such stories produce their response by striking some very basic chords in human nature. The story of the 'Corrupt Magistrate', of course, is no more than a reflection of the whole history of human corruption; that power corrupts is an observation which has become proverbial, and its truth can be demonstrated by a glance at virtually any daily paper. But the particular pattern of events dramatized by Shakespeare seems to have been based on an actual mid-sixteenth-century case near Milan involving a Spanish count or captain. This anecdote was given various renderings in the sixteenth and seventeenth centuries, sometimes with the circumstantial details of the date, 1547, the ruler's name, the judge's nationality, and so on. But the fact that the story was given a contemporary setting in these versions is probably no guarantee of its authenticity, though undoubtedly this was one of its attractions insofar as its moral implications and applicability were concerned. It is common for folk tales to become attached to particular individuals, or anchored in particular places, for life often imitates art, and it is traditional for story-tellers not only to vouch for the truth of their fictions, but to establish it by the provision of suitable circumstantial detail. Swift amusingly parodies the method at the beginning of each book of *Gulliver's Travels*.

Poetic justice has a universal appeal; to see a man hoist by his own petard, to see someone who richly deserves it get his comeuppance, to see ego deflated, these demonstrations are all irresistible so long as they are not happening to us. But apart from the often very deeply-felt desire to see justice triumph, to see the dog have his day, to see the little man vindicated and the overbearing brute brought low, such stories have a rich comic potential. Thus in Shakespearian comedy the whirligig of time does bring its revenges, as in *Twelfth Night*, where Malvolio's early sneers at Feste are very suitably dealt with later, and the enemy of cakes and ale is made a laughing-stock.

But one of the attractions of comedy for most human beings is surely that it allows us to enjoy vicariously those thumbings of the nose at authority, those well-aimed pies in the eye of pomposity, which in real life are so rarely possible. As Miss Prism (quite unaware of the implications of the sad truth) reminds us in *The Importance of Being Ernest,* it is in fiction that the good end happily and the bad unhappily. In real life things are different, frequently consisting of those timeless human experiences catalogued by Hamlet:

> Th' oppressor's wrong, the proud man's contumely,
> The pangs of disprized love, the law's delay,
> The insolence of office, and the spurns
> That patient merit of th' unworthy takes.

In comedy these problems can be, and have been, entertainingly solved at the expense of the oppressor, the egotist, the human iceberg, the swindling or dilatory law and lawyer, the insolent office-holder and the vain but ungifted. In the everyday world this is not managed quite so readily. In fact, like the poor, the problems enumerated by Hamlet are always with us.

In the story of the 'Corrupt Magistrate', one version of which forms the core of *Measure for Measure*, we have the best of both worlds—a serious depiction of genuine injustice which is ultimately resolved, plus the comic, or at least ironic, working out of poetic justice. This combination naturally lends itself to tragi-comic treatment; the real injustice promises potentially tragic consequences, which in a different kind of play might well have developed, but the comic form of this play ensures a different conclusion.

However, that the final outcome depends not so much on the nature of Shakespeare's raw materials as on the form within which he chose to work, is readily recognized if one compares the basic situations of *Romeo and Juliet* and *A Midsummer Night's Dream*, two plays written at about the same time. Both plays share the initial situation of parental disapproval, which threatens the lovers' happiness and even their death. In *A Midsummer Night's Dream*, a comedy, Theseus warns Hermia that if she does not comply with her father's wishes and marry Demetrius, her fate will be:

> Either to die the death, or to abjure
> For ever the society of men.

The dire consequences of her ensuing elopement are avoided through the intervention of magic and moonlight, though in the different context of *Romeo and Juliet* a similar flouting of parental wishes leads to catastrophe.

But if the notion, dramatized by Cinthio, Whetstone and Shakespeare that it is best to do to others as you would be done by, is of ancient lineage, stories of monarchs who went about in secret among their people to discover abuses and correct wrongs, are equally widespread in world folklore. And the comic possibilities of someone not knowing the true eminence of the disguised person are immediately apparent. They were employed at least as far back as the classical myths in which the gods visited earth in human form, and in Britain recur (to choose two examples at random) in the story of Alfred burning the cakes or Richard the Lionheart being given a drubbing by Robin Hood.

In Elizabethan drama rulers in disguise were popular figures on the stage, as in *Fair Em*, *A Knack to Know a Knave*, *George a Greene* and others. In Greene's *Friar Bacon and Friar Bungay* the Prince of Wales in disguise woos the Fair Maid of Fressingfield, while in *Henry V* a more serious function is served by Henry's disguise and visit to his troops on the eve of Agincourt.

107

This motif of slumming, of going down and out in London, and its comic possibilities, is also encountered in *Henry IV,* where Prince Hal for a while upholds the unyoked humour of Falstaff's idleness among thieves and tapsters, and in Rowley's play *When You See Me You Know Me,* where Henry VIII wanders at night through disreputable parts of London, meeting the same kind of people that frequented the Boar's Head tavern. But as W. W. Lawrence has pointed out in his *Shakespeare's Problem Comedies,* the motif was used differently in Jacobean drama to allow the contemporary questioning of values. In Marston's *The Malcontent* and *The Fawn* and in Middleton's *Phoenix,* fictitious Italian dukes in disguise are used as vehicles to castigate the vices of court and country. It should be remembered here that *Measure for Measure* is a Jacobean play and that indeed, though we naturally think of Shakespeare as the greatest Elizabethan dramatist, most of his major tragedies and all of the late romances were written after the death of Elizabeth. Shakespeare is in fact the greatest of the Jacobean dramatists.

As with the disguised ruler, so with the bed trick: it was a familiar device of folklore and needs no apology. Shakespeare had used it previously in *All's Well That Ends Well,* and although it may offend some modern tastes, its use in *Measure for Measure* is both theatrically effective and (from a Jacobean point of view) technically proper. Under English common law a declaration by both parties that each took the other as spouse was legally binding, whether it was later consecrated or not. Angelo's declaration of intention to marry Mariana at some future time was not binding, and he repudiated it because of the loss of her dowry. However, such contracts automatically became full marriages in the eyes of the law if intercourse occurred. With the Duke's encouragement and Isabella's help Mariana succeeds in converting the contract. The legal arrangement is given moral justification by the Duke:

> He is your husband on a pre-contract:
> To bring you thus together 'tis no sin,
> Sith that the justice of your title to him
> Doth flourish the deceit.   (IV. i. 72–75)

These matters are treated sensibly by J. W. Lever in his introduction to the New Arden edition of the play (1965), which is to be preferred to the old-fashioned view outlined by Quiller-Couch in the New Cambridge edition (1922). Lever, however, fails to make the connection between Isabella and the 'Patient Griselda' story. The latter is essentially a moral exemplum in which the heroine displays astonishing constancy when it is put to a formal test. Helena in *All's Well* belongs to the same tradition and, in that play, the commonly-attendant motif of the 'impossible condition' is also present; Bertram will not recognize her as his wife until she is pregnant by him. In *Measure for Measure* Mariana's desertion by Angelo allows her to display her constancy in traditional fashion, but more particularly Isabella, for whom she acts as substitute, may also be seen as successfully undergoing a test which proves her worthy of marriage to the Duke. It is Isabella, not Mariana, who is the centre of the play, and her marriage to Vincentio is not, therefore, to be condemned as the mere provision of a partner necessary for the final processional exit of happy couples with which Shakespearian comedies usually end. Seen against the tradition to which Isabella belongs, her marriage to the Duke is inevitable from the start, as much a *donnée* as the Duke's reason for appointing Angelo his deputy, which the critics have argued about and which Shakespeare never explains because it is irrevelant to his main concerns.

Isabella combines two traditional characters of Elizabethan romance and drama, the subject lustfully pursued by her prince, such as Margaret in *Friar Bacon*, Ida in *James IV*, Rossalin in *John of Bordeaux*; and the wronged heroine, such as Dorothea in *James IV*, Angelica in *Orlando Furioso*, and Iphigina in *Alphonsus, King of Arragon*, all plays by Robert Greene. Similar characters appeared in Greene's prose fiction: Barmenissa in *Penelope's Web*, Bellaria in *Pandosto*, Sephestia in *Menaphon*, and Isabel in *Never too Late*. It should be remembered in this connection that Shakespeare knew at least one of these works: *Pandosto* is the source of *The Winter's Tale*. That he may have known some of the others is at least suggested by the fact that Greene was the first critic of Shakespeare, labelling him 'an upstart Crow beautified with our feathers.'

This is not to suggest that Isabella is a cardboard Griselda, or an allegorical figure from the Morality plays, a Chastity personified, or Forbearance or, in the play's last scene, Charity. She is clearly more complex than that. But not enough attention has been paid to the theatrical and literary traditions which went to her making, and I am not as convinced of the absolute psychological reality of her character as many critics seem to be. One cannot disregard either her exemplary function in the play, or the traditional nature of the materials of the play itself, and in reading the critics' comments about Isabella one is constantly reminded of the extravagant praise that has been heaped on the heroines of Greene's plays, who have been praised for their realism and pointed to as foreshadowing some of Shakespeare's women characters. In fact, however, they are not three-dimensional at all, but are little more than personifications of feminine virtue.

The difference between the genius of Shakespeare and the second-rate talents of a Robert Greene is manifested by the way in which even Shakespeare's basically generic characters usually take on a vividly conceived individuality: Pistol does not remain only a Miles Gloriosus any more than Angelo is only an allegorical figure of Puritanism, Hypocrisy or False Authority. But this commonplace should not prevent us from seeing that some of Shakespeare's characters are more realistic than others who remain primarily functional, the Duke in *Measure for Measure* being an example.

That we still talk about all of Shakespeare's characters equally in terms of psychological realism shows how difficult it is to escape from established critical fashions and habits of thought. The expansive nineteenth-century novel taught critics and readers to expect psychological probing in depth, and the Shakespearian criticism of A. C. Bradley reflects this expectation and obsession. Concentration on the minutiae of character development has led to critics treating fictional dramatic characters as though they have an existence outside the limits of the play, and this habit has been re-enforced by the advent of psychiatry, so that the inevitable consequences have been books and essays which treat plays as though they were the records of psychological case studies. Some of the resultant absurdities are discussed by L. C. Knights in his famous essay, 'How many children had Lady Macbeth?' Not surprisingly, the tragedies, with their introspective soliloquies and probing of motives, have lent themselves more readily to this treatment than the comedies, but even here the quest for realism has led to the invention of non-existent problems.

In recent years films and television have strengthened our assumptions about the necessity of realism in stage sets, costumes, properties, dialogue, and naturalistic acting, though these trappings often disguise the highly conventionalized nature of the formula plots and the absolute unreality of both character and action in most suburban situation comedies. It would probably not occur to those who seriously question the ethical propriety of the bed trick in *Measure for Measure* to ask about the implications, in a television serial, of an American Air Force officer who shares his quarters with a scantily-clad eastern beauty who issues from the spout of an Aladdin's lamp.

It is obviously possible, if not all too easy, to ask the wrong sort of questions about certain kinds of drama all of which, if it is to work, demands our acceptance of certain variable conventions. It is for this reason that I have concentrated on the theatrical and literary conventions which contributed to *Measure for Measure,* and on the pattern and structure of the play rather than on the motivation of its characters. It can easily be demonstrated that to discuss the reality of the plots of Shakespearian comedy is absurd; a glance at them shows at once how preposterous they are. Think for a moment of the caskets plot in *The Merchant of Venice* or about the pound-of-flesh bond itself. As someone has said, they have no more reality than Jack and the Beanstalk. The same is true of the law against fornication in *Measure for Measure*— deriving from the source as it does, it is a *donnée* which only a puritan such as Philip Stubbes could accept as realistic.

But the death penalty, the bed trick, and the disguised Duke are as necessary to the play as Cinderella's glass slipper is to her story, and such unrealistic details can be made the occasion of extremely moving theatrical episodes, horrific, tender or beautiful. We probably recognize immediately that the stories in *The Merchant of Venice* of the caskets, the pound of flesh, and the beautiful young girl disguised as a wise young judge cannot be measured in terms of modern realism, but this does not prevent us from responding to one of Shakespeare's most romantic and at the same time, significant plays. This should also be true of *Measure for Measure* if we do not misunderstand the kind of play it is, for of course it too follows the basic pattern of romantic comedy, in which the course of true love never did run smooth.

In comedy, and particularly in romantic comedy, conventions determine to a large extent the behaviour of characters and the structure of the play itself, which moves towards a predetermined end—the festive conclusion, usually involving the marriage of the principal characters. Even as the play opens we know that eventually Jack shall have Jill and all shall be well, but before that event can occur, conventional obstacles of the sort enumerated by Lysander and Hermia in *A Midsummer Night's Dream* (I. 1. 134) have to be overcome. Just as inevitably as in *As You Like It* or *Twelfth Night* or *Much Ado About Nothing,* the plot of *Measure for Measure* consists essentially in preparing the main characters for marriage. While it is true, therefore, that *Measure for Measure* is also a drama of ideas and that, as Professor Lever says, 'the play is profoundly concerned with major intellectual issues', to reduce the comedy, as is so frequently done, to a dramatized debate on the themes of Mercy and Justice, Grace and Nature, Creation and

Death, Seeming and Reality, the Old Dispensation and the New, Authority and Truth, Liberty and Law, Dissolution and Fertility, is to over-emphasize its didactic intent and to deny its dramatic power, its comic content and its romantic flavour. The issues just listed (some of which Mary Lascelles examines in her level-headed book about *Measure for Measure* published in 1953), are of course raised in the play which is, nevertheless, a true comedy, as Shakespeare's fellow actors and first editors rightly saw.

Angelo, Isabella, Lucio, the Duke and the rest must be seen, then, as existing only within the context of *Measure for Measure*. They are fictional characters moving within the very formal conventions not only of a poetic drama, but of a particular dramatic genre, and it is fruitless to discuss them in terms of psychological realism. It is in a highly selective way that they demonstrate certain modes of human action, for the world of comedy is also unrealistic in that it generally excludes much that real life contains. Even in *Measure for Measure,* which is orchestrated in such a way that a great variety of moods is achieved, and over which the threat of death hangs menacingly, we know from the start that the duke's disguised presence ensures that ultimately all will be well.

We must neither overstress the moral significance of *Measure for Measure* nor overlook its variety of humour. The dim-witted-ness of Froth, the malapropisms of the Dogberry-like Elbow, the clownish jokes of Pompey, unimpressed by authority, and who in typical Shakespearian fashion is given one of the play's truths to speak, namely, that to achieve Angelo's reforming aims would necessitate the gelding of all the youth of the city, all help to relieve what might otherwise be an unrelieved gloom. And Barnadine's refusal to die for any man is comic, though in its own way, like the incompetence of constable Pompey, it also shows that the Law is an ass. Claudio, who is now prepared to die, will do so unless the Duke intervenes, but the incorrigible Barnadine is saved by his determination to remain drunk. Lucio's ribald wit also provides its peculiar flavour, and his exchanges with the disguised duke allow us to laugh at Vincentio's discomfiture and should prevent us from taking him too seriously as a symbol of divine providence.

The play provokes other responses as well as gleeful chuckles, broad laughs or wry smiles: sympathy for, and perhaps irritation at Isabella; shock and probably relief at the revelation of Angelo's clay feet—it is too formidable to contemplate a man whose urine is congealed ice—and a sentimental appreciation of Mariana's fidelity, helped by the mood music of the song at the moated grange. But finally the play comes down on the side of tolerance, and of a measured justice that recognizes the reality of human imperfection. As in Shakespeare's other comedies, we have been shown that ideal love must be based on self-knowledge, and that it is in any case only one variety of an emotion which can also be ridiculous, pathetic, coarse, misplaced, agonizing, transitory and commercial. But it is to be celebrated, for human love is a necessary pre-requisite for individual happiness, political stability and the preservation of the natural order. It is for this reason that Juliet's pregnancy is seen as a natural good, not only as the natural outcome of an ideal love, but as a promise of the continuance of the great cycle of death and rebirth which Shakespeare was to celebrate so gloriously in his last Romances. It is for this reason that Lucio is given those beautiful and quite uncharacteristic lines in which her pregnancy is described in terms which link it with the harvest riches of the turning seasons:

> As those that feed grow full, as blossoming time
> That from the seedness the bare fallow brings
> To teeming foison, even so her plenteous womb
> Expresseth his full tilth and husbandry.   (I. iv. 41–44)

And it is for this reason that the obstacles to true love which must be overcome before Jack can have Jill are therefore necessary in *Measure for Measure*, not only to provide the basic plot of Romantic Comedy on which Shakespeare has erected this particular and unique superstructure, but also to establish the supreme value of that love which his play celebrates as a rejuvenating force. As Eve asks in *Paradise Lost*, 'And what is Faith, Love, Virtue, unassayed?'

THE LANGHAM REGIME

Herbert Whittaker

The history of our theatre has depended heavily on memory, not records—we pore over gushy personal reminiscences by old players for a hint of how their theatres were run. We probe behind these flowery autobiographies for a glimpse of the men who held these actors together in a company.

At the risk of seeming precipitate I decided to set down a few observations about the years Michael Langham spent at Stratford. It is too soon to make any exact estimate of his great contribution —and one certainly has no wish to push him into Stratford's past—but the Langham years repay immediate attention—for their own interest and for fuller enjoyment of this first season under new management.

Michael Langham entered Stratford to music. That is to say, the first music festival was held in 1955, the year the thirty-three-year-old English director was invited to assist Tyrone Guthrie. It was a pleasing omen, but did not mean that his association was to be entirely free of discords.

Langham's contribution to the Stratford Festival and to this theatre is so great that it need not be enhanced. That accomplishment must not be diminished by any notion that he came fully equipped with the knack of the difficult stage, or the difficult Canadian actor.

Michael Langham faced antagonism, even rebellion in his early years as director here—for he had to bear the terrible onus of replacing the father-figure of the Festival, Tyrone Guthrie. It was presumed that Langham was a protégé of Guthrie's. Langham remarked later that they had met but seldom before Stratford. He had been brought over on the strength of his work abroad.

Michael Langham's first interest in theatre was as an actor, at university and while reading for law. In London, he slipped away from the Law Courts to perform at the little Arts Theatre. Then came the war and its great and terrible influence on the Langham career. For five years, Langham was incarcerated in a German prisoner-of-war camp. It turned him from a promising lawyer into an experienced stage director. He experimented 'with every play in the book', he remembers, while he 'concentrated on not being bitter about it.' After the war, he had decided on his career. He went to the Midland Theatre Company, working out of Coventry. It was there he married the gifted comedienne, Helen Burns. In the German camps, Langham had directed a number of Canadians in his productions. But this didn't make things altogether easy when he came on to Canada.

Guthrie's choice of Langham as his assistant and eventual successor was actually his second. His first lieutenant from the beginning of the Festival had been Cecil Clarke, who had emerged from the war as its youngest brigadier. Clarke performed wonders of administration and organization but was less successful when Guthrie turned over to him the 1954 production of *Measure for Measure*. Guthrie had to step in at the end to help calm the actors.

This general dissatisfaction of the company with anybody but Guthrie was transferred to Langham when he started work on *Julius Caesar* in 1955. The actors still revered Guthrie and were jealous of any successor who might take his place. It was very much an expression of the Canadian actors' immaturity at that time that they were soon in open rebellion.

Langham's fault, in their eyes, was that his methods of directing were as different from Guthrie's as was his temperament from that of the tall Irish-Scot. The new man directed in a most meticulous fashion, compared to Guthrie's inspirational style. One of the actors, David Gardner, expressed the difference thus:

> I was cast as the poet who pokes his nose into the tent scene in *Julius Caesar*. I asked Michael how he wanted the tiny role played. 'Play it', answered Langham, 'as a symbol of degeneration!'

That might be a useful phrase in a review of a performance but not in the creating of one, Gardner felt. But as he emerged through the tunnel, Guthrie leaned over to supply an answer: 'A scarecrow, dear boy, a scarecrow.' 'Tony worked like an architect, Michael like a painter, with meticulous brush-work.' And he further unsettled the actors by reblocking and reblocking scenes.

The actors had a meeting, their first of any kind. Langham was invited. He heard the complaints. He remained very cool. The

Canadian actor in those days needed to love someone so desperately. For them, Michael was not lovable. Later, they were to change their minds, and cling to Guthrie's successor as passionately as they had to Guthrie.

Outsiders recognized something of the situation. 'Michael Langham is bound to suffer endless comparisons with Tyrone Guthrie', I wrote at the time, 'all of them unfair. He is a different kind of director, certainly less spectacular, less of a spell-binder for the actors, but surprisingly able to summon excitement to the Guthrie stage.'

This was true of the first Langham production, *Julius Caesar*. His difficulty with the actors showed in performance, but Shakespeare came to his rescue. The Forum Scene with Lorne Green as Brutus and Donald Davis as Mark Antony, was rousing stuff. Langham had deployed his mob throughout Stratford's tent-theatre and we found ourselves becoming part of the Roman uprising. The death of Cinna the Poet was equally arresting. Cinna was dismembered completely and the mob left the stage empty. And the final glimpse of Antony and Octavius exchanging baleful glares across a darkening stage made a chilling finale.

The actors started to change their minds about their new artistic director the next year when Langham set to work on *Henry V*. First of all, his concept was particularly exciting for Canadians. And so was his choice of Henry. The combination quite overshadowed Langham's other production for 1956, a most respectable showing of *The Merry Wives*.

Christopher Plummer had been recommended to Tyrone Guthrie when he was first auditioning in Montreal. The Montreal actor was reported as unruly and Guthrie rejected him. But since 1953, Plummer had been doing well on Broadway. Langham liked him and decided that here was his Henry. Here indeed was Langham's principal player in the next decade.

Plummer was an exciting king. And opposing him were other exciting actors, one of whom was to be as important to Stratford. Langham was fascinated by the differences between French and English-speaking Canadians. He had seen *Le Théâtre du Nouveau Monde* and wanted to use their kind of theatricality to ginger up the established company. He may have found Guthrie's choice of actor earnest but dull.

So he invited Gratien Gelinas, Quebec's leading comedian, and members of the *Nouveau Monde* company, Jean Gascon, Jean-Louis Roux, Guy Hoffman, to play the French court. The contrast of personalities and playing-styles made Langham's

1956 *Henry V* most electrifying. It had special meaning for Canadians, one which they discovered was not necessarily shared abroad. When at the end of the season Tyrone Guthrie took the company to the point of origin for its revolutionary stage, the Assembly Hall at Edinburgh, the English critics saw no point in having the French court speak broken English.

Langham's success, coupled with that of Guthrie's *Oedipus Rex* at Edinburgh, won him respect all around. His opinions began to be listened to, though sometimes with shock. 'The Festival is a freak,' he pronounced publicly. 'It will grow arid and die unless the native Canadian theatre develops and expands.' At another time, the *Globe and Mail* took editorial exception to his declaration: 'Shakespeare should not be taught in schools. It is unwise to submit such plays to bookish theories or class-room study unconnected with the stage.' At another time, Langham risked calling down the wrath of the harvest gods when he criticized the constitution of the Canada Council.

But everybody respected Michael Langham by 1957 when the Festival reached its great moment of security, when it moved in to occupy the unique cement structure which had been erected, under enormous pressures of all kinds, to replace the tent.

In that year, Michael Langham, as artistic director of the Stratford Festival, naturally directed the first play, which was just as naturally *Hamlet,* with Christopher Plummer as the prince. And it was only proper that Tyrone Guthrie should be invited back to direct *Twelfth Night* as the second night's production.

The theatre rather overshadowed the *Hamlet,* Plummer notwithstanding, but Guthrie restored the balance with a dark comedy version of *Twelfth Night,* one which was quite staggering in its focus, not on the rollicking of Douglas Campbell and Plummer as Sir Toby and Sir Andrew, but on the sour old clown that Bruno Gerussi made of Feste.

Having accepted the Stratford Festival as possibly here to stay, the citizens of Stratford came to recognize Michael Langham as a good neighbour. If he dropped in, he could be very amusing. But when the next set of productions got under way, he again became aloof, never looking to the left or the right but keeping his mind entirely on the job. He sat up nights, it was known, worrying about what he would do with a certain scene the next day. He liked to have everything down on paper before rehearsals, the actors explained.

Langham had learned how to command his actors. By 1957 it had been reported that if he got really angry about something you could hear his voice down at the Avon. 'And he could chew out a day-dreaming actress like a liverish drill sergeant', it was said. 'Perhaps I am a little too ostentatious', Langham confessed, 'but there's nothing I can do about it if I'm going to do the job as successfully as I know how.'

And successful at that job he was certainly becoming. In 1958 he and George McCowan staged the earthy *Henry IV, Part One*, and even better was his *Much Ado About Nothing*, with Eileen Herlie come to play Beatrice to the Plummer Benedick. This *Much Ado* was a sumptuous, satisfying production, and people began to speak less of Guthrie's mastery of the stage. It came after an effort to expand Stratford and affect the Canadian theatre outside its boundaries, in which Langham lost a little of his newly-gained prestige.

Stratford had ventured on its first tour and its first original script before the regular season. Shakespeare's *Two Gentlemen of Verona* and Donald Harron's adaptation of Von Kleist's *The Broken Jug* went out to Toronto, Montreal and New York but unsupported by the magic of the Stratford theatre did not impress the public unduly. Langham, who had directed both productions, smarted under the bad notices and poor business. He refused to account the productions as failures. 'We are never allowed to forget our unsuccessful tour', he complained in 1959, and stated his opinion that Canada's proprietary view of Stratford was parochial.

The year was a sabbatical one for Langham. He had refused an offer from the Old Vic that year, counteracting any impression that the Langhams were not really rooted in Canada. By this time he was in command at Stratford in every respect. In 1957, he had been made general manager as well as artistic director. Victor Polley was named assistant general manager and comptroller at the same time. But Langham's health had started to suffer from the burden. From his days in prisoner-of-war camp, Langham retained physical conditions that were to give him severe pain. He was hospitalized in New York, and his visitors there found in him a man who had brushed up against the possibilities of death.

Michael Langham changed as a director, and there were many reasons for it. One must remember that he came to Stratford suffering still from the torture of the years in prisoner-of-war camp. He was a very up-tight man, as we say now. And he was not physically well. The physical pressures brought him to a point of crisis in 1958, when he was hospitalized and when he faced death. This period had a profound effect on him, and on his work.

While its artistic director and general manager was absent on grave matters, Stratford had to console itself with Peter Wood's production of *As You Like It* with Irene Worth returned to play Rosalind, and the joint Jean Gascon-George McCowan production of *Othello*. Douglas Rain's Iago and Kate Reid's Emilia were much admired but Langham was certainly missed.

He returned, sufficiently recovered to direct an ambitious production of *Romeo and Juliet,* as if his experience had made him more ready to tackle tragedy. He had originally hoped to indulge his old interest by making the Capulets French-Canadians, and had sought Leslie Caron as his Juliet. When she was unavailable, he chose the American star, Julie Harris, to play opposite Bruno Gerussi's Romeo, and dropped the Quebec connection entirely. The production was not a great success. Nor was Douglas Seale's *King John,* starring Plummer. Seale had run into the same kind of rebellion that Langham had encountered early in his Stratford days, and there was much smoothing-over to be done.

But the shy young Englishman with the prisoner-of-war background had grown into a true leader of a great company. He had developed as a diplomat. He became adept at handling actors. He could smooth the ruffled feathers of visiting directors with charm and fast talk. He also handled the board of governors brilliantly, it was reported.

1961 was to usher Stratford and Langham into a great period. His *Coriolanus* of that year brought Paul Scofield to Canada and his *Love's Labour's Lost* brought another favourite, Zoe Caldwell. Miss Caldwell, whom Guthrie had discovered at Stratford-upon-Avon the previous year, was summoned to replace Toby Robins opposite John Colicos in *Love's Labour's Lost.* That *Love's Labour's Lost* was one of Stratford's most exquisite achievements, the finding of a bright new treasure on a dusty shelf. It revealed a new mastery of the Stratford stage for Langham, topping his earlier *Much Ado About Nothing* in the same vein.

That season Langham again experimented with an original Canadian play, Donald Jack's *The Canvas Barricade.* This modern satire, which George McCowan directed, was the result of the Stratford-Globe and Mail Competition, for which Peter Ustinov, Robert Whitehead, William Inge, Michael Langham and I were the judges, so I got to know Langham better and to explore his involvement with Canada. He would sit listening while I burbled on about Canada's need to establish its own drama, as if he were a bright-eyed animal peering out of his burrow. He always seemed on the verge of understanding this vague conceit called Canadianism. Certainly he was working towards it, even if *The Canvas Barricade* didn't do much to establish it.

Love's Labour's Lost was followed in 1962 by a most successful showing of *The Taming of the Shrew,* with Colicos and Kate Reid, and then in 1963, by *Troilus and Cressida*: sly, wicked and very funny. The *Shrew* had shown off Langham in a new and freer spirit, and this was matched in the same year by the romantic splendours of *Cyrano de Bergerac,* with Plummer again to the fore as the long-nosed hero. Opposing these two was a dark and turgid *Macbeth,* directed by Peter Coe, with Plummer and Miss Reid as the pushy couple. Trouble broke out again in the ranks, the reception to *Macbeth* nearly splitting the company.

The problems arising from this *Macbeth* were to put a special strain on Langham, for he had risen from his sick-bed for *Love's Labour's Lost.* He felt the need of change at Stratford. 'One always leaves a place when it's doing well', he said, 'it's the process of re-creation.'

With this in mind, Langham had chosen Peter Coe, the thirty-one-year-old Briton who directed *Macbeth,* as his successor. Langham insisted that Coe's bad notices for *Macbeth* and the resultant friction would make no difference. Coe was invited back to Stratford to direct *Timon of Athens,* in 1963.

Then Coe reneged, and the burden of the extra production fell upon Langham. It didn't stop *Troilus and Cressida* from being another witty Langham success but it did no good for *Timon of Athens,* which Langham felt bound to stage with the designs decided upon by Coe. Despite Colicos's compelling interpretation, this *Timon of Athens* had an unsatisfactory showing.

But Colicos came resoundingly into his own the following year—and so did Langham as a director of tragedy—when they tackled *King Lear* together with Leslie Hurry as designer. The wide recognition of Langham's mastery of Shakespearian comedy had been accompanied by some reservation about his, and indeed Stratford's, ability to stage any of the tragedies with full success.

The *Lear* was to give this rumour the lie. It was altogether a monumental achievement, austere and painful in its great design. And to show that he had lost none of his comic touch, Langham also produced the high Restoration romp of *The Country Wife* in the same 1964 season, with Mrs Langham (Helen Burns) in the title role, Douglas Rain as Pinchwife and Colicos as Horner.

That year was a year of great Stratford triumph. Being the quadricentenary of Shakespeare's birth, the company had been invited to England to take part in the celebrations. The original hope was for a showing at the Old Vic, but this was transferred to Chichester which was more suitable because its theatre is based on the open-stage concept of Stratford's now-famous design.

Langham took the opportunity to refurbish *Timon of Athens* and make it work for him. He revived, and who can blame him, the delicious *Love's Labour's Lost*. The Chichester programme was completed by Jean Gascon's *Le Bourgeois Gentilhomme*.

Langham fought furiously to get the right conditions for his actors abroad and they in turn delivered everything he wanted, winning much acclaim for themselves, for him and for Canada. Their return was no less heart-warming, for the *King Lear* was widely recognized as a great accomplishment.

Langham took another sabbatical after this triumphant year, leaving the direction to Stuart Burge, John Hirsch and Douglas Campbell. His departure may have been spoiled a little by a silly incident. He had planned to make a short speech from the stage on the last night. For some reason, some of the actors protested. Hurt, Langham gave up the idea. The speech—the first from the stage—had to be made by William Hutt.

Hutt is one of the actors who has come up to great distinction under the Langham regime. Although the criticism of never really leaving England followed Langham to the end, he had developed and promoted the Canadian actors at Stratford—Hutt, Rain, Colicos, Plummer, Kate Reid and Frances Hyland—and they became bigger names because he believed in them. He also supported the Canadian directors—Gascon, Hirsch, McCowan and Douglas Campbell, a Canadian once removed. From his importation of Desmond Heeley in 1957 he had developed new and brilliant designers.

That year of the *Lear* was to prove the peak of Langham's regime. There were some stormy seasons ahead. One disappointment came when he had to abandon his prized scheme to complete the Shakespearian canon and play all the histories, as only the Royal Shakespeare Company had done.

The board of governors eventually pointed out that Canadians did not seem to share his passion for Britain's early history and Langham dropped the project within easy reach of the end, jumping from *Henry VI* in the Barton version to *Richard III* to make a centennial full-cycle.

His 1966 revival of *Henry V* was somewhat of a disappointment too, for viewers objected to his forcing this patriotic work into darker passages. There is always the cry of 'distortion' when a director attempts to make a classic work fit the mood of today.

Perhaps the urge to follow this course indicated that Langham was again impatient to move on, was feeling the need to conquer new fields. I contend that a director who stages a pertinent classic seriously as a classic cannot help but present his contemporary view of it. When he starts consciously to stretch the original out of shape to have it express his own comment on his times, he does neither himself nor the classic much honour. So it seemed with Langham's second *Henry*.

He ran into more drastic trouble that same season of 1966, when he ventured into the field of new work again. William Kinsolving, an American writer, was invited to make a play for Stratford's second stage, the Avon, on the subject of the collapse of the Romanoff regime. Tried out in Winnipeg, at the Manitoba Theatre Centre, the Kinsolving work was found wanting in theatrical values. In heroic effort Langham turned to a Stratford dramaturge, Michael Bawtree, and invited him to supply another text on the same theme, employing the same physical production. *The Last of the Tsars* proved much more palatable, but Langham's hope of taking it on to New York, to Broadway, never materialized.

There were compensations, of course. Langham's television version of *Henry V* for CFTO, Toronto, was a beautiful job of translation and the old history regained vigour in colour on the screen. Previously, in the year of the *Shrew* and *Cyrano de Bergerac,* Langham had brought a group of Canadian actors to American television in *The Affliction of Love,* also much admired.

By 1967, it was made known that Langham would accept the invitation to build a new theatre in La Jolla. His season for Canada's centennial would be his farewell one as artistic director. For just such an occasion, Langham had saved up one of the most exciting works of the entire Shakespearian canon, *Antony and Cleopatra.* This would be coupled with *The Government Inspector* by Gogol, and Canada would see Stratford on tour and at Expo, appearing there among the great companies of the world, including Sir Lawrence Olivier's National Theatre which supplied its competition at another Montreal theatre.

It is perhaps too early to trace out any grand designs, or mark any significant ironies in the Langham story but it is inescapable when you go over the record, even swiftly, not to notice certain peaks and valleys.

It was Langham's discovery of Christopher Plummer which helped win him the respect of Stratford and put him on the way to being accepted as a true successor to Tyrone Guthrie. It was the same actor's delay which took the edge off this swan-song production of *Antony and Cleopatra*.

Planned as the major work of the centennial season, it had to be postponed until late in the summer because of Plummer's film involvements. When he finally arrived, the actor was pressed to catch up with Zoe Caldwell, his Cleopatra, and the other actors. Langham gave in to him in sympathy but the finished product, at Stratford and at Expo, missed its potential greatness.

It is to be hoped that the successors whom Langham named, Jean Gascon and John Hirsch, will soon persuade their illustrious predecessor back to the scene of those early and middle triumphs. Michael Langham took the stage which Tyrone Guthrie had created and against odds pushed it into new usage. His subtlety and delicacy of interpretation have certainly given Stratford some of its greatest productions. When any man has tamed this sly and stubborn platform his skill must be retained, for the list of directors who have already tried it and failed, or partially failed, is remarkably long already.

For Canadians, Michael Langham stands as the last colonial governor of Stratford, the one who brought it and its actors towards new independence. Already we have seen productions this year, in the Festival Theatre and at the Avon, to make us confident that Langham chose his successors well. Jean Gascon and John Hirsch are as unlike Michael Langham in style as he was to Tyrone Guthrie. Their contribution is as distinctive. We need them all for Stratford.

'MY CROWN, MINE OWN
AMBITION AND MY QUEEN'
(ON PLAYING CLAUDIUS)

Leo Ciceri

When you see a production of a play do you ever wonder how certain things in it, or even the total concept of a production came about? This discussion will range from the first days of rehearsal of *Hamlet* way back in January, before the tour, until we opened the show here in Stratford. Some of these remarks may make some of the qualities in our production richer and more understandable.

There is, I'm sure, no Shakespearian production that starts with a single conception and goes right through to the finish without a change. I do know of one director, with whom I worked in England (you can look up his name if you are really interested) who tried to do it that way, and it was fascinating to watch him work. In one production of *Coriolanus* starring Tony Quayle there was an entrance where the director wanted him to stop at the foot of the left stairs on an entrance, and the scene was blocked that way. Then one day, perhaps after a solid breakfast, Tony felt that the impetus of the entrance should take him to centre-stage. The director agreed. However, at the next rehearsal of the scene it was, 'Tony, dear boy, I think it would be much better if you were just two paces back,'—the following rehearsal, 'Tony, dear boy, if you could manage to be just one step back', and Mr Quayle was right back there at the foot of the steps again. But this is rare in directors. At the end of 1960 I can remember Michael Langham showing me a complete set of designs for the next year's production of *Love's Labour's Lost*, set 1910–1913. For that brilliant production, the first in which he felt he had conquered this stage, Mr Langham saw the play as a statement of the last days of youth and the beginning of maturity. What better time than the late glow of the Edwardian era about to disappear into the mud and misery of the first great war, not to mention the humour he could foresee in the movements of the ladies in those impossible hobble skirts? How they would have got up and down the stairs is impossible to imagine. Perhaps they would have hopped? In any case the opportunity to find out never arose because when we assembled in April the costumes had been changed by Michael and Tanya Moiseiwitsch, the designer, to Velasquez and sixteenth-century France. Why, I was never quite sure. This changed the quality of movement a great deal and led to the enchanting swirl that gave a delicious feminine note to that lovely production of *Love's Labour's Lost*.

Our director of the present *Hamlet* saw the play in essentially modern terms and the first set of costumes was modern. Then perhaps because there have been many modern dress *Hamlet's* or perhaps because he felt that a modern interpretation of the play would be more striking against an earlier age, the designs were changed to early Renaissance eleventh- and twelfth-century Denmark, with overtones of the Byzantine Empire. Set in wintertime the true chill of Denmark was to be carried through with furs and leather. Of course the designs aren't absolutely authentic but interpreted with a modern eye by Sam Kirkpatrick. (One thing I'm sorry about in the transference from the proscenium stages of the tour to the great thrust stage of this Festival Theatre is the loss of a dark brown cyclorama, which was merely a background for some scenes, but for the court scenes was lit from behind to give the effect of great stained-glass figures.)

These were the designs we saw when we arrived late January to start rehearsals for the tour. On the first days of rehearsal here there is always a model of the set with the changes and additions for the scenes and the costumes pinned up on boards on the stage. With *Hamlet* there were no set changes but for *Measure for Measure* there were the great doors and the steel floor which we had to give the whole play something of the ambience of a prison. When the cast looks at the costumes and the set, the director then gives a talk outlining the basic intentions of the production, and character notes. With the feeling from the costumes and the set, and these seminal ideas, you begin to work on the play. (One director who did not do this was Tony Guthrie who started straight in on the blocking without even a read-through of the play. Some directors feel that everybody should hear the play through at least once because they suspect—unfortunately they are right—that some actors will read only their own parts.) Our *Hamlet* was outlined as follows. It was to be as pertinent and timely as possible. Denmark, cold, dank and somewhat drunken, under Claudius, was a fascist state with the people murmuring and the students in rebellion. The first scene was to begin with a student attack on the palace, to be driven off by Claudius's soldiers. Political prisoners were engaoled or driven into exile. (I must confess that I was a shade startled by this description of the opening, especially of Claudius as fascist, but as we all work out of our personal feelings and backgrounds I questioned our stage director at that time. He is Hungarian, and he said, 'but of course, all kings are bad. Whenever we had a good one we immediately made him a saint!') Polonius had made it possible for Claudius to murder his brother the king, and had perhaps even connived at it. So that Claudius was a sort of puppet king with Polonius and Gertrude running the kingdom. Whenever Polonius wasn't with him, Gertrude was. All the ages were brought down from where they are usually played. Hamlet is in his late teens, early twenties, an appropriate age for a student despite the textual note that he is thirty. We have altered the grave-digger's speech so that the age around twenty seems correct. When Michael Langham did the play before with Christopher Plummer he worked with the idea that the play took over ten years and that Hamlet was away for a long time, so that he started at twenty and ended up thirty. Depending on the length of time Hamlet is with the pirates the play takes between three or four months unless you allow for a very long time away. One university student viewing our simple and speedy production came to the conclusion that the play took two days. Gertrude and Claudius are in their early forties, Polonius in his late forties. Hamlet, then, becomes a modern youth, acting out of the romantic idealism of late adolescence rather than someone caught in the pressures between actuality, a sensitive awareness of the compromising and lying about him, and his personal sensitivity to the demands made upon him by his feelings and the ghost's revelations. It's very much the attack by youth against the establishment. One moment of this can be clearly seen in the handling of the 'seems, Madam, nay I know not seems' speech of Hamlet's. It's not used as a self-revelatory speech but rather to castigate the court for their lack of respect and mourning for the late king. Ophelia and Laertes enter into this picture of youth, with Ophelia, by her love for Hamlet, sympathetically aware of the chicanery of the world and distressed at the behaviour of her elders; and Laertes, a chip off the old block, already a sell-out to the establishment. Polonius, instead of being a wry, shrewd politician just beginning to fray about the edges, emerged as a much more forceful person. For example, the first court scene began with Polonius handing

Claudius a speech, which Polonius had prepared, to be read off as a public pronouncement.

With these general ideas we read the play and started work. After about two and a half weeks we had a run-through. Things began to emerge and the play started to shift ground. The student rebellion was never staged because of the evidence of the first scene. Bernardo asks Francisco, 'Have you had quiet guard?' (wondering if the ghost had appeared to him as well). Francisco answers, 'Not a mouse stirring.' It wasn't considered wise to interpolate, 'save for the lowly anti-establishment students shouting below.' Later in the scene Marcellus's question about the reason for this 'same strict and most observant watch', is answered by Horatio's explanation of the political situation and the threat from Norway and Fortinbras. Had Elsinore been seen to be under the threat of some modern student activists there would have been every need for a strict and most observant watch, and no explanation necessary.

There was a great deal of consideration given to the text in the pre-tour rehearsals. The director wanted to find a more simple and direct statement of the play and so cut some of the more elaborate passages of emotional writing. In Hamlet's soliloquy, 'O what a rogue and peasant slave am I', the section from 'am I coward' to 'about my brain, I have heard' was dropped, leaving out all the bit about 'or ere this I should have fatted all the region's kites with this slave's offal', etc. In Claudius's prayer scene the emotional turmoil of 'O bosom black as death', etc, was cut. The intention throughout was to remove from the text what might seem extravagances against a sharp, clear and simple statement of the play, 'simple' in the sense of anti-Shakespearian.

I can remember being told that the scene with Gertrude after the closet scene should have the quality of Strindberg. There is now a movement from England of a new style of playing Shakespeare. The Royal Shakespeare Company found a certain hardness and clear ring for the handling of the text in their great history cycle *Richard II* to *Richard III*. This new style is the latest one in the constant revolution, or evolution, in Shakespearian production. The greatness of the author is that (to mix metaphors) he is there like a rock to sustain practically anything and, deeper than ever plummet sounded, his ground will never be reached.

William Poel, early in the century, went back to the text played with only a few props and a curtained surround, stripping the stage of the extravagances of the Victorian productions of Irving and Beerbohm Tree. Whole scenes in those productions would be cut to make room for a tableau with no words illustrating the scene, or the stage would have live rabbits hopping about and deer tethered here and there. (The poor actors who have to work with animals: I can remember the shrewdness of Michael Langham's use of animals in *The Taming of the Shrew* here. The lord of the hunt and his party were in green and we had three most beautiful golden retrievers come on with us. It was gorgeous, and the audience paid no attention to the actors but went 'ahhh' and were immediately brought into the play in a very sympathetic fashion.)

Gielgud and a group around him, Dame Edith Evans, Peggy Ashcroft, Gwen Franccondavies, Michael Redgrave and others created in the thirties the *beautiful* Shakespeare. I was lucky enough once to play Aumerle to Gielgud's Richard II, and this beauty I speak of had nothing pretty about it. There was great elegance of thought and speech and gesture. It was right for its time and, though it may not have had the guts so much in evidence today, its sensitivity, its depth and the music were incredible. I feel that it is dangerous to use a constant style for all of Shakespeare's plays. Guts and clarity are an absolute essential for the historical plays where poetry has been superseded largely by excellent dramatic verse (excluding *Richard II*), but what do we do with *Twelfth Night* and *The Tempest,* to mention two? Now back to our production of *Hamlet*. It belongs to the modern school, owing something to Jan Kott, the Polish author of *Shakespeare, Our Contemporary,* the political ambience concept. There is one possible merit that follows from cutting the more purple sections of poetry, the production (for example, the recent Nicol Williamson-Tony Richardson production) can become a starring vehicle for a fine actor. But to cleave solidly and straight-forwardly to the story line and to unravel the interplay of the full cast of characters is to get down to the bed-rock of the play, so that the brilliance of the playwright rather than the supreme ability of some one actor is in evidence. I wonder if ever there could be assembled a full company of actors where, with a full text, the total picture of *Hamlet* could be given. I think the audience would leave the theatre touched and overawed as they have never been.

We finished our rehearsals and went to Chicago for our tour opening. Most of the play continued as it was but I was having troubles with Claudius. I was a-straddle two stools. The original reading of the role had undergone changes, (he now was a little more in command of the kingdom) but it had never been fully rejected, and I was groping toward something combining it and a new Claudius. Audiences help a great deal. Shakespeare was such a true dramatist that audiences sometimes know better than the actor the direction in which the play or the part should go, and with a kind of seventh or eighth sense the actor allows himself to be steered into port. The first year I was here, 1960, the production of *King John* opened badly because of personality conflicts, but by the end of the season it was vying with *A Midsummer Night's Dream* as the best of the three productions of that summer. *Richard II* when it opened wasn't clear or solid. In fact I can remember on the first night, as I exited as Henry IV following the corpse of Richard, one white-jacketed gentleman sitting in the front row sighed with relief, 'it's over', but by the end of the season it was standing cheek by jowl with a magnificent *King Lear*. This was as a result of the sensitivity of the company to the audiences, and happened in the days when the plays opened here absolutely cold, without a tour.

In any case, with one eye on the text and an ear to the audience and the groupings that we had, things began to happen to the Claudius/Gertrude/Polonius relationship. Polonius's awareness of the murder had been long since dropped and the emotional relationship of Claudius and Gertrude came more to the fore. Polonius remained a powerful advisor to the king, but Claudius ran Denmark and the physical closeness of Claudius and Gertrude, instead of being political, became a statement of their love—one of the main reasons Claudius carried out the murder.

We returned from the tour and the cast was enlarged and costumes were added and some changed. Sterner and more sober ones were provided for me. I was half sorry to lose one costume. It was an enormous red fox-fur cape, a stunning colour, and the audience certainly didn't look at many other people on the stage when that was around. Suggestively it was good in the prayer scene, all that you could see of me was my head and hands, the rest of me dripping with blood. Nice, but just a shade distracting; with the blaze of red you just couldn't see my face. That costume was one of the most wonderful upstagers in the business.

We worked on the play, clarifying ideas and moves and reblocked it for the thrust stage. Some of the original ideas remained from January. I still had two soldiers as my personal bodyguard from the beginning of the play. Shakespeare has one line indicating special soldiers for Claudius, late in the play, immediately before Laertes arrives on the scene to demand retribution for his father's death. Claudius calls out, 'Where are my Switzers, let them guard the door.' This is a brilliant touch, coming after Claudius is certain Hamlet knows he is the murderer and has sent Hamlet to England. Claudius is afraid for his life, but because Hamlet is so beloved of the Danish people he hires Swiss mercenaries as his personal bodyguard. In this production the line is deprived of some of its value because of the political orientation at the beginning. The prepared speech handed me by Polonius was struck, and Claudius became a much more autonomous figure. Ophelia retained her political awareness and dislike of the Claudius/Gertrude/Polonius faction. Fortinbras became a fascist, a statement carried out in his costume —black leather reminiscent of the SS troops. Hamlet and Laertes continued in the same line on which they had begun in January.

All through rehearsals the director had been adamant against speechifying in a desire for absolute simplicity in the speaking and statement of the text, and about half-way through our rehearsals we had a run-through that was a most fascinating experience. There had been no general talk prior to the rehearsal about how we should go about it, we just started and went through the play. I now call it our 'Zen' rehearsal because with only two or three people in the auditorium the whole cast was imbued with one spirit and merely played the play, or rather let the play play them. It was a quiet performance, at times people could not be heard in the eighth row. It was slow, but such was the depth of concentration on the stage that time in an ordinary sense ceased to exist for the people watching and only the time of the play was real. We were told after it was over that it had been a tremendously moving experience and that the statements of the characters became crystal clear. The motivations in the case of Hamlet and Claudius, for example, became so sharp that a tremendous tragic tension was created since it was impossible to square one against the other as right or wrong, because both were seen as men caught by pressures that forced them into the actions they followed. It became our real world.

I remember Graham Greene on the Third Programme in England saying that the book that had influenced him most was *King Solomon's Mines*. 'This may seem odd', he continued, 'but you see, it was the first book in which I realised that the world was not black and white but grey and dark grey.' During the play, although there is a good personal reason each time, Hamlet does either kill or cause to be killed five people while Claudius has only killed one, despite the fact that he makes several attempts to do away with Hamlet, only achieving it at the end of the play. After the 'Zen' rehearsal which contained the kernel of the show we now present, the rehearsals continued, clarifying and pointing the straightforward quality of the production.

Now I feel rather like the actor in a production of *Twelfth Night*, with great characters like Olivia, Viola, Orsino, Malvolio, Belch,

Feste and Aguecheek, who when asked what the play was about said, 'well, you see, there's this gardener's boy called Fabian . . .' I'll let you guess which part he played. Our play is *Hamlet* but I'm going to talk about Claudius.

Shakespeare gives many clues in his work but some of them are given in a sort of negative way so that sometimes you have to go by indirections to find directions out. In the first scene of *A Midsummer Night's Dream,* for instance, we have Theseus interrupted in his wooing of the captive Hippolyta by the claims of Egeus for control of his daughter, Hermia. At the end of the scene Theseus does a strange thing—he exits taking Egeus and Demetrius with him leaving the two lovers, Hermia and Lysander, alone together. Why does he do this? To me it seems that he does this to let them plan their elopement. He is a conquering king who has carried off his bride and he wants to find if the love of Lysander and Hermia is strong enough to take them out of Athens. He does say two things in the scene which suggest his intentions to me. First he is aware of Demetrius' wooing of Helena and says, 'I must confess that I have heard so much and with Demetrius meant to speak thereof', and in the same speech he says to Hermia, 'look you arm yourself to fit your father's fancies or else the law of Athens yield you up.' Is there not here the negative suggestion that if you are *not* in Athens you are safe? He leaves the choice to the lovers, but suggests to me his own awareness of their real love and a hope that they will elope. In a production here I would like to see Theseus come out on the top balcony and listen happily to the lovers planning to leave, and have Hippolyta observe this so that, if there were any doubts in her mind about her future happiness they are banished by the knowledge of this gentleness and recognition of true love in her captor. With Claudius there are many clues as to how and why he did what he did. The ghost appears in his habit, as he lived, as an armoured figure. The descriptions of him include 'our most valiant brother', 'such was the armour he had on when he the ambitious Norway combated', 'so frown'd he once when, in an angry parle, he smote the sledded Polacks on the ice.' Hamlet senior seems to have been a king who spent a good deal of his time fighting to protect or extend his lands. Also in his return as a ghost he would choose the most recognizable form possible, not to waste what little ectoplasm he has, and so he comes with martial stalk in his armour from top to toe. This suggests to me that he was seldom at home, and that the running of the kingdom and the chairmanship of the privy council was left to his younger brother, Claudius. This explains the close relationship between Claudius and Polonius, the ease in electing Claudius to the kingship after the sudden demise of Hamlet senior; the handling of the office is already in Claudius's hands and with the pressures from Fortinbras it would be wiser to continue on rather than let young Hamlet take over, who, away studying in Wittenberg, would not be up-to-date in all the state problems. Hamlet senior's frequent army manoeuvres also account to me for the conjunction of Gertrude and Claudius. Hamlet's speech 'why she would hang on him as if increase of appetite had grown by what it fed on', has sometimes been used to suggest a very passionate Gertrude but I feel it simply states the emotions of a generous woman, affectionate and happy to have her man safe and home from the wars. God knows how soon he will be away again. With that the case, we have a beautiful woman spending long lonely hours wandering around Elsinore and spending quite a few with Claudius, either having meals together or discussing some point of statecraft until between them grew a love, on Claudius's part a deep love, which eventually led to adultery. I think he did the murder to gain *power* and *Gertrude* and they are inseparable in his mind—'My crown, mine own ambition and my queen' is one line in the text. I don't think it was an easy step for him to take, but he was actually in charge of the running of the kingdom and had begun a serious affair with Gertrude. His older brother's return always interrupted further growth and so he took his advantage in the orchard and did away with him. Gertrude was probably greatly saddened by Hamlet senior's death, but also happy to marry Claudius to assuage her guilt over her adultery and make her an honest woman. It was with these ideas in mind that I began to approach the role on our return from the tour. A strong, clear-minded ruler who is essentially a statesman-king rather than a warrior-king, Claudius resolves the affairs with Fortinbras with an embassage and an exchange of letters, supporting his suggestion that Fortinbras doesn't encroach on Denmark with the strength to back it up should the need arise; and a war is averted. His guilt over the murder is under good control, and he hopes time will smooth all things. His relationship with Gertrude is at this moment complete, only blurred by the disgruntled attitude of her son. Hamlet's behaviour he puts down to the sudden death of his father, his mother's hasty marriage and the loss of the election to the kingship. Claudius is strongly aware of Hamlet's closeness to his mother and is careful not to mention the marriage when he criticizes Hamlet for his extended mourning. For Hamlet and for the Court the marriage has been a political one to solidify the kingdom in treacherous times. When next we meet

Claudius, two months have gone by during which time Hamlet has become more and more extravagant in his behaviour until two school-mates of his, Rosencrantz and Guildenstern, have been summoned to jolly him into some sense and also perhaps to find out for Claudius whether or not there is anything more to this madness than meets the eye. Gertrude believes it is because of his father's death and their o'er hasty marriage, Polonius that it is from frustrations of love, but Claudius's guilt is beginning to sharpen his intuition. His 'we shall sift him,' and his query to Gertrude 'do you think 'tis thus?' indicate to me a man who is entering a lonely area where his guilt will finally separate him from mankind. He will ask questions and judge the responses but his ideas he will keep to himself; once Claudius has committed the murder I don't think he truly has one quiet moment. The first scene with Rosencrantz and Guildenstern is the closest he comes. The embassy to Norway has been successful; surely Rosencrantz and Guildenstern will discover something; hopefully nothing about the murder. Perhaps even Polonius has the answer. Gertrude and he are still close.

Then comes the nunnery scene. All of Claudius's fears explode into vivid life. Hamlet's words claiming that he is revengeful and ambitious, and that those that are married already 'all but one' shall live, attack Claudius on all three fronts. Hamlet intends in one sharp action to reverse the world as Claudius has made it. By killing Claudius, Hamlet will revenge his father's murder, attain the throne and release Gertrude from what Hamlet sees as the bondage of her marriage to Claudius. It is always dangerous to interpret simply one character's reference to another. Shakespeare never loses sight of the character's own bias and personality at the moment, and all statements have to be sifted. Claudius, though the plan to have Hamlet murdered in England is only half formulated in his mind, knows that there will be no peace in the kingdom until Hamlet is removed from Denmark one way or another. It is at this moment that I feel Claudius enters into the action of the play proper. All his other actions took place before the play began and until now he has only watched and waited until he knew his ground. The play scene follows, and Hamlet laughs in his face in his attempt to expose him. During the mimed play Claudius sees that Hamlet knows of the crime and he tries to bluff it out, but something in the death throes of the player-king rips open a sealed moment in his memory and he sees his crime for the first time for the thing that it is. He truly feels the agony of the brand of Cain on his soul. From this moment on the play gradually strips

Claudius naked. The prayer scene which follows I consider to be the crux of the part. Without it I'm sure that Claudius could be played as an out-and-out-villain—even as Angelo in *Measure for Measure* could be played as a hypocrite were it not for two soliloquies; when in one he describes his struggle, in the other his remorse. We have already had one note of remorse from Claudius, 'O how smart a lash that speech doth give my conscience,' when Polonius tells Ophelia to read her prayer-book to camouflage the reason for her appearance to Hamlet. This is cut in our production. However, in the prayer scene we see a man who once could pray, facing his spiritual destitution. His crime—for his crown, his own ambition and his queen—has driven him to a position from which there is no return and he must plod on carrying the burdens of them all. He then goes to the queen's bedchamber to have news of her interview with Hamlet, seeing that Polonius hasn't come to him. The murder of Polonius shocks him with the awareness of just how dangerous Hamlet has become, but more than that he discovers that his relationship with Gertrude can never be the same. The intensity of his love will remain but henceforth they will be separate people. In our production Gertrude does not believe Hamlet's accusations of murder and is not trying to protect him from Claudius in that sense. Rather she tries to protect Hamlet from the legal results of the murder of Polonius, on the grounds that he is truly insane. Claudius realizing what he is about to do and how deep her love is for her son, knows that one of the main things for which he murdered Hamlet senior, his love for Gertrude, will now be denied him. Referring to their ill-advised laxity in controlling Hamlet, which has led to this murder, he uses words which are a double-edged knife—'we would not understand what was most fit, but like the owner of a foul disease to keep it from divulging let it feed even on the pith of life.' This is the recognition of the second loss in his life. First the murder has bereft him of his spiritual life, now the ramifications of it have separated him from his beloved wife. The next short scene is the climactic scene of the play, Hamlet and Claudius face-to-face for the first time with complete awareness on both sides. There has been some cutting at the end of the scene. Delicious things to say like, 'do it England, for like the hectic in my blood he rages and thou must cure me,' have gone. However, following the cuts, it is now possible for me to suggest that Claudius is forced much against his will to attempt the murder of Hamlet. The possibility that Gertrude will find out is one reason why it is to be carried out in England. Claudius is not an inveterate murderer but now he knows there will be no peace for him or the kingdom as long as Hamlet lives. He is not a Macbeth who strikes out at Banquo and Macduff to protect his crown after the murder of Duncan. Claudius is a different human being.

The next scenes in which Claudius is involved is the scene of the rebellion of Laertes, and Ophelia's mad scene. His crown, the last remaining thing that he sought is now in jeopardy. He has great control in this scene with Laertes because he is on absolutely safe ground, but Ophelia's madness is to me in an abstract sense the state of the kingdom. Everything that seemed complete has lost connection, and though the words make sense the continuity is lost. Her songs also ring with criticisms of his behaviour, albeit unconscious on the part of Ophelia: 'Quoth she before you tumbled me you promised me to wed,' touching the adultery of Claudius and Gertrude. Then at the end of the scene it is almost as if truths are coming to him from a world elsewhere—'and will he not come again, no, no, he is gone, go to thy death bed, he never will come again.' 'God have mercy on his soul and on all Christian souls, I pray go,' I think sounds a knell in the mind of Claudius and he wishes to turn time around, but cannot. From here on the only things that keep him going are his now unrequited love for Gertrude and a meagre desire for self-preservation.

The original text has the king plot the murder of Hamlet with Laertes immediately after the arrival of Hamlet's letters and before the willow speech. But the plan of the unbaited rapier and the poisoned cup has in our production been placed after the burial of Ophelia. It is useful for Laertes because his compliance now comes after he has seen the murderer of his father, and endured the burial of his sister. However, in the previous scene with Laertes as we now have it the whole scope of the relationship between Gertrude and Claudius is scanned. From the plangent statement, 'as for myself, my virtue or my plague, be it either which, she's so conjunctive to my life and soul that as the star moves not but in his sphere, I could not but by her,' to after the willow speech when Laertes leaves, the queen stands there drained of emotion. During rehearsals there grew a look between Claudius and Gertrude which suggests the enormous separation between them and the drudge their lives have become. Now it seems that the rupture between them is complete as the queen moves more and more towards her son. When Hamlet appears at the graveyard Claudius is forced to face the inevitability of his position and makes one last attempt to destroy him by initiating the plan with Laertes. I feel that by now he realizes that it is hopeless, and that it is only a matter of time before retribution will strike. There is no security for Claudius after Hamlet has declared, 'the cat will mew and dog will have his day.' He does not set his own guard, as that might warn Hamlet, but tells Gertrude to care for her mad son.

The last scene of the play has the king and queen make the same entrance as for the first court scene, but with a marked contrast for now there is a separation, the weight of their experience is upon them and Claudius is aware of the intended murder in his heart. When finally by signalling the cup to Hamlet he places it handy for the queen to drink and brings about the destruction of the only thing he loves, Claudius, though alive, has reached the end of his life. When he sees in Gertrude's eyes the accusation, 'the drink, the drink', he is destroyed—except for one moment of attempted self-preservation and hatred for Hamlet who has brought it all tumbling upon his head. His crown passes to Fortinbras who in this production will rule with all the constraint of a dictator. His own ambition instead of power politics between great kingdoms has become a cat-and-mouse game with Hamlet. His queen has been destroyed through his own machinations. Is Claudius a villain, or a man who has committed one foul deed and lives to see the destruction of everything for which he committed it?

SHAKESPEARE IN THE NEW WORLD

Murray D. Edwards

The title of this paper, *Shakespeare in the New World,* has, as many titles, a certain amount of ambiguity in it. What is the subject matter? What does it imply? Well, I might as well confess immediately: you are not going to be regaled with stories about William Shakespeare's experiences in the New World. I wish that were possible. Imagine the consternation among scholars if they were faced with irrefutable evidence that Shakespeare had once stepped on these shores. Now that would surely be an original topic for a Ph.D. candidate!

Shakespeare, of course, didn't come to North America; that sort of adventure apparently wasn't appealing. But his plays did. Restless English actors did travel to this new part of the world in the early days and most frequently they had one or two Shakespearian plays in their *repertoire.* And he is still very much with us, in a grander fashion, as is evidenced by the Stratford Shakespeare Festival in Ontario, to say nothing of the proliferation of other Shakespeare Centres in the United States and Canada.[1]

So, in this paper, we will consider some of those plays of Shakespeare's that were brought over from the 'old country' in the early days. And we will be mainly concerned with plays which were performed rather than those which were published in this country. Although I may dwell on the Canadian scene, I have no intention of disregarding events in the United States. Indeed some interesting differences appear when we compare certain aspects of a Shakespearian production. Interpretation, points of emphasis, deletion of scenes, addition of scenes, audience reactions etc., are noticeably different in one country as compared to another. This is significant

---

1 See Saturday Review, June 1968. Some of the major summer theatres in the United States and Canada listed by Henry Hewes are: American Conservatory Theatre, San Francisco, Calif.; American Shakespeare Festival Theatre and Academy, Stratford, Conn.; Asolo Theatre Festival, Sarasota, Fla.; Champlain Shakespeare Festival, Burlington, Vt.; Minnesota Theatre Company, Minneapolis, Minn.; New York Shakespeare Festival, Central Park, New York; San Diego National Shakespeare Festival, Baboa Park, San Diego, Calif.; Stratford Shakespearian Festival of Canada, Stratford, Ontario; Oregon Shakespearian Festival, Ashland, Oregon.

in that it says something about the countries. Shakespeare becomes a sort of barometer! So, I suppose a reason for this little exercise, apart from unearthing production details about Shakespeare, would be to throw some light on that old conundrum, Canadian cultural identity. Is the Canadian really just a half-hearted American? Is there anything distinctive about a Canadian that sets him apart from his 'cousin' south of the border? Personally, I'm beginning to believe there is a great deal of difference. Having done the research for this paper, I feel much more confident in my conviction that we have in these two countries two separate cultures. My thinking was first influenced, I must confess, by the seemingly insignificant fact that Shakespeare's reception was different in the two halves of North America.

Shakespeare, early on, was very popular and generally dominated the stage in the United States, but in Canada this was not the case. He was presumably well respected but not at all conspicuous among the playbills of the time. On the other hand, he was a great influence on a particular aspect of Canadian playwriting, namely the poetic drama, but this influence though laudatory on the surface was, as far as I can discern, detrimental to the growth of the drama in this country. To understand why he was unpopular and how, in my opinion, he contributed to Canada's 'weary, stale, flat and unprofitable' drama, we must turn to the past and observe some theatrical events.

Information about Shakespeare on the stage in the United States and Canada is not overly abundant. As usual we know more about the theatre in the United States than in Canada, and I am particularly indebted to Esther Claudman Dunn who, in her *Shakespeare in America,* has given us an excellent account of Shakespearian activity in the various regions of early America.[2] As for Canada, I have generally been forced back on my own resources.[3] Hopefully, however, I have accumulated enough information to allow us to draw some tentative conclusions with regard to Shakespeare's impact in the two major halves of the New World.

We might begin by examining one large subject area—moral

2 A more recent book which covers generally the same ground in a lighter vein is Nancy Webb and Jean Frances Webb, *Will Shakespeare and His America* (New York: The Viking Press, 1964).
3 Most writing about theatre in Canada is naturally concerned with contemporary events. Much of the information about performances can be found in the following books:
Hector Charlesworth, *Candid Chronicles* (Toronto: Macmillan 1925).
Murray Edwards, *A Stage in our Past* (Toronto: University of Toronto Press, 1968).
Walter McRaye, *Town Hall Tonight* (Toronto: Ryerson Press, 1929).

acceptance and rejection as it operated in Canada and the United States. One obvious point that becomes evident in the early stages of research in the so-called North American Shakespearian Theatre is that in the beginning the attitudes are almost entirely derivative. For the American the step is back to England. For the Canadian it is sometimes a one-step, sometimes a two-step. He either sought the attitudinal beginnings (by that I mean style, moral objection, schools of thought) in England or in England and the United States. It is rare, in the early days, to find an original attitude in the United States, and never, to my knowledge, will you find one in Canada. The United States followed, imitated or mimicked the English tradition for years. Canada filled the role of 'follower' of England and the United States until recent times.

The opposition to the theatre that was quite consistent in the United States in the period previous to the revolution was, as Esther Claudman points out, 'exactly like the opposition that Shakespeare faced in his own lifetime.' As we know, the hard-nosed businessman puritan insisted that the theatres be built outside the city limits. The same sort of reaction was prevalent in the New World. There was, in other words, a general feeling of opposition to the theatre that stemmed from the mother country and we should consider it natural to find puritanical resistance in pioneer America. We note, of course, that the underlying reason for moral opposition in the beginning in America was derivative. This gradually changed, and the reaction, no longer essentially moral, gained a particular colour, one that became consistent with the culture of the United States. Moral, social and political reactions tended to blend and a more definitive attitude, which reflected American temper, emerged.

As I have said in the beginning, American opposition to Shakespeare was puritanical. There is ample evidence to indicate that. The most difficult ground for the thespian was probably Boston—the 'banned in Boston' expression being well known right up to our time. But in America, the puritan force was diminished considerably following the war. After the blood had flowed, the moral temper cooled, and as it cooled a liberal attitude toward the theatre began to form. America was, at this time (1790s), beginning to be conscious of its own social and political identity. It is my contention, in fact, that this period—the turn of the eighteenth century into the nineteenth century—was a crucial one for the development of the American theatre.

The same period in Canada witnessed the bare beginnings. Puritanism far from disappearing gained in importance becoming,

I suspect, the respectable rampart raised for protection against what appeared to be blatant immorality south of the border.

In this period of puritanical opposition the method of dodging the morality squads was essentially the same in England, the United States and Canada. The best way to fight the puritan was on his own ground: the most popular method, therefore, was the 'moral lecture' approach. The piece, usually written by the playwright but occasionally by a concerned public figure, was presented to convince the playgoer of the moral worth of stage shows. Sometimes the whole prologue was devoted to the cause. One that I found to be a rather touching tribute to the theatre was written by a prominent Philadelphian on the occasion of Douglass's first performance on Society Hill in 1759. He said in part:

> To bid reviving virtue raise her head
> And far abroad her heavenly influence shed;
> The soul by bright example to inspire,
> And kindle in each breast celestial fire.

Then he added the inevitable offering to the puritan:

> So may each scene some useful moral show
> From each performance sweet instruction flow.

A few years later, when Douglass was in New York, he felt obliged to publicize his production of Othello as:

> A series of Moral Dialogues in Five Parts,
> Depicting the Evils of Jealousy and other
> Bad Passions, and Proving that Happiness
> can only Spring from the Pursuit of Virtues.

We can understand something of the strength of the puritan fibre in Canada when we observe that a similar moral tribute was made in Canada in 1898. The mayor of Montreal opened Her Majesty's Theatre with an address, and one or two lines in a poem which he had possibly written for the occasion caught my eye:

> That all we offer shall be clean and Pure,
> Immodest scenes admit of no Defence
> For want of Decency is want of Sense.

This time lag with regard to moral rejection in the United States and Canada is worth remarking, and we should note that it is caused in part by the difference of intensity. The Canadian's refusal to accept a more liberal attitude toward the theatre was strong and lasting. Plays that were accepted in the United States still ran the gamut in Canada years later. Ibsen's *A Doll's House* stands as an example. When it had become common with the little theatre groups in the States, in Canada it was still being seriously rejected by the public and the critics in the commercial theatres. This delay pattern is a fairly constant factor which must be taken into consideration when making comparative studies of the theatre in Canada. The persistent Canadian puritanism maintained the cultural lag and, obviously, created a climate that was quite different from that in the United States. The injection of Shakespeare into these two cultures reveals some of the differences.

In America, Maurice Morgann's prophecy of Shakespeare's future in the 'New World' (and here he obviously meant that part of the New World that would become the United States) was borne out. He said in part, 'When the hand of time shall have brushed off his present Editors and Commentators' (reference here to people such as Voltaire who dared call Shakespeare a barbarian) 'the Appalachian mountains, the banks of the Ohio . . . shall resound with the accents of this Barbarian.' There is little doubt of Shakespeare's popularity in the United States. Shakespeare was constantly produced in the settled cities of the east and the little towns dotted along the ever-expanding frontier.

Now, as many theatre historians point out, it would be comforting to make the argument from this evidence that the survival of Shakespeare was proof that greatness will triumph. There is a good deal of truth in this, of course, but when you focus your attention on a society, you discover other reasons why a great playwright is accepted or rejected. It strikes me, therefore, that it would be worth our while to consider some of the reasons why Shakespeare would be popular, or not so popular in a pioneer country. The reasons are quite obvious but I think throw some light on our examination of the cultures in the United States and Canada.

No doubt we can assume that Shakespeare was popular in the United States partly because of the wealth of finely-wrought characters in his plays and the beauty of his language. We could also argue that his plays were adaptable to a necessarily wide variety of stages. And from a sociological point of view we must note that his plays provided an excellent vehicle for declamation, which Americans generally loved, expressed a primitive vitality, which they admired, and represented the fashionable society of England, which they took pains to imitate.

But when we consider the last three points in relation to the Canadian scene, we are forced to a different conclusion. (To start with, we must remember that the moral resistance was more sustained and, as I have noted, affected the general climate.) Taking the points in order we find that Canadians, on the whole, were suspicious of declamation, so this would certainly not stand as an important assurance of popularity. The vigorous primitive vitality? Here we find that suspicion hardens into an out and out rejection. Canadians, by and large, and here I am generalizing outrageously—but must to make a legitimate point—sought constantly to reject primitivism in their environment. The ideal of being civilized ladies and gentlemen—although living in raw nature—was constantly in their hearts. The cruder aspects of Shakespeare offended their sensibilities.

In Saint John, New Brunswick, in 1816—for example—we find that some actors had formed a new company. They produced Saint John's first Shakespeare, *Romeo and Juliet*. The newspaper man suggested that this new company possibly over-played its hand in trying to revitalize the theatre in this city for, as he said, 'Such plays of allegedly ribald nature prompted another flood of letters to the editor.' There was a demand for the mayor to take action.

In 1877 in Toronto we discover that 'for the first time in Canada' Shakespeare's *Cymbeline* was produced, with Adilaide Neilson as Imogen. The reviewer noted that the 'plot turns upon an incident which is of rather too strong a flavour to agree with the delicate not to say squeamish stomachs of modern audiences.'

I don't want to hammer at this point too much, but I must say that in my research I have been constantly reminded that Canadians have not, in the past, been favourably inclined to crudeness, vulgarity or primitivism, ingredients found quite often, as you all know, in great art. So Shakespeare was not really welcomed with open arms on the Canadian stage; a quite different picture than in the United States. In Halifax, in the early days—according to an article, 'Early Halifax Theatre'—he was actually unpopular. Not many of his plays were acted and these probably were never presented more than twice. *Catherine and Petruchio* or *The Taming of the Shrew* was given two performances, *The Merchant of Venice* was acted once and formed with *The Citizen* the first bill of the New Theatre. The celebrated comedy called *The Tempest* or *The Inchanted Isle,* another revision, and *Richard III* complete the list.

The particular reason for Shakespeare being unpopular in Halifax is not easy to discover. It was probably directly related to the three points we are now discussing: the disinterest in declamation, the fear of primitivism, and the complete lack of desire to appear fashionable simply by demonstrating an appreciation of Shakespeare. Canadians didn't want political independence as history has told, and maybe because of that felt no pressing desire to act like Englishmen, to feel superior by an outward show of adulation. It is possible that they didn't feel the need; they were English, Shakespeare was English, and that was the end of it. It was surely not considered showing off or bragging for the Canadian to be seen at the theatre where Shakespeare was playing. But Canadians weren't innocent of this human fault. We find them seeking status in their society by being seen at large and extravagant American musicals.

This business of fashion plays an interesting part in the development of a culture. Too much emphasis seems to lead to a form of caricature, while the absence of it produces a society that is more difficult to identify. The American's concern about fashion grew partly from his opposing attitudes toward democracy and aristocracy. Everyone knows the dilemma; the freedom the Americans sought in their democratic way of life was the freedom to 'get ahead'. They insisted on the right to rise to an aristocracy. And, of course, the English model was constantly there to cause alternating feelings of worship and disdain. Shakespeare was admirable and it was, therefore, fashionable to be seen at one of his plays. And yet this same audience could envy and hate the Englishness that Shakespeare represented. There was a tension that was not present in the Canadian psyche and as a result, as I have tried to show, Shakespeare's impact was minimized. This general reduction of intensity in the social and political spheres is probably somewhere at the base of any theory we may wish to develop as an explanation of Canada's mediocrity in the theatre.

Although Americans presented and witnessed plays by Shakespeare because, to a great extent, it was the fashionable thing to do, this did not inhibit their reactions in any way. Shakespeare was great; everybody knew that! He was also on the open market, and in America that meant no holds barred.

As a result we find Shakespeare sharing the stage with the most extraordinary collection of riff-raff and trash. Shakespeare's plays were cut up, rearranged, transplanted, played in rag-time. Charming local touches were inserted whenever the occasion offered itself. I noticed on one occasion that 'Richard III was appropriately accompanied by a song in celebration of Washington and Liberty.' And there was the funeral procession in Romeo and Juliet being 'enlivened' by Handel's song, 'Return O God of

143

Hosts'. *Hamlet* while being played in Charleston in 1795–96 was 'given a new Parlour Scene executed in a most masterly fashion.' The desire for the unusual in Shakespearian productions included, on one occasion, an acrobat who danced 'the much admired Spanish Fandango, blindfolded over thirteen eggs, playing The Castanets.' Local jokes, of course, were often slipped in between the lines.

Shakespeare was rarely given the chance to have the evening to himself. The Shakespearian play was either preceded or followed by short skits or plays. I noticed a reference to a performance of *Henry IV* that was followed by 'a grand ballet, and a farce written by a gentleman from the town.'

After-pieces of 'trash' were quite common. In Philadelphia in the winter of 1831–32, there was apparently a 'spirited protest' when *Richard III* terminated at the end of the third act because of the actor's asthma. Something called *The Evil Eye* was substituted and the audience managed to sit through it. But when the curtain went up on the after-piece, a farce called *Raising the Wind* we read that 'some gentleman black-guard threw a large piece of plaster extracted from the roof of the pit passage, with some force upon the stage.'

A chap by the name of Noah Ludlow introduced an interesting wrinkle to the business of producing Shakespeare in the west. He was apparently facing a financial crisis when he teamed up with a circus manager to offer 'a combination of dramatic and equestrian performances.' He opened with this arrangement in Cincinatti with *Catherine and Petruchio*. Whether bare-back riding was introduced as a legitimate part of the performance or merely served as interval material is not clear. All sorts of visions I'm sure are coming to your mind.

Shakespeare was dumped right down on the American stage and had to fight for his life, and during the fight Americans tested themselves. The playwrights made their ridiculous first stumbling steps; maybe one of those ghastly farce after-pieces. The actors, in many cases, at first imitated the English actors until they found their own voices and intonations. 'Imitations', in fact, were very popular in the United States in the early 1800s. You came across items like this: 'Mr Duff will give imitations of celebrated performers: Mr Kemble as Hamlet, Mr Cooke as Richard III', etc. In 1823 the American actor, Wallach, consented to present in public imitations of Mr Kemble as Coriolanus, Mr Kean as Richard III, etc., and so all sorts of exciting experimentation went on.

But in Canada, the theatrical activities pale in comparison. Extraordinary events, and amusing incidents are not easily found. The country is more sedate, and the reflection in the theatre bears this out. We should note, however, that something of that sedateness—conventionalism? the respectable bordering on boredom? —is a bi-product of the touring company, and Canada received most of its theatre from foreign touring companies. Touring was (and is) a business. The idea is to sell to the most people, and there is, therefore, a tendency to shape productions so that they will have a popular appeal. The public is to be wooed not shocked. American and English touring companies obeyed these rules. As a result productions of Shakespeare's plays, and others, tended to be conventional, rarely breaking from the tradition of the time.

There were one or two exceptions, of course. Ben Greet stands out. The unconventional aspects of his productions were ideally suited to Canada. In fact, it would seem that because of his particular style of presentation he avoided the United States in favour of Canada as his compatriot Frank Benson did.

F. R. Benson, you may remember, was the English Shakespearian scholar and director who spent his life in an effort to realize a rather wistful dream: the confederation of the English-speaking people of the world through the influence of Shakespeare. Benson gave up the United States after a performance in Chicago where the critics' reviews were rather unkind. Greet restricted his activities generally to Canada.

But why? That isn't easy to answer. There was an all-pervading 'Britishness' about these groups. They had a tendency, possibly, to look down the nose at the peasants. But there is also the fact that Shakespeare was presented as a study. The flair and grandeur, the 'show biz' qualities were definitely excluded, and Americans wanted a 'show'. Canadians were apparently more inclined to be studious.

Greet, possibly following the lead of Benson, sought to simplify the production of Shakespeare, to seek out the Elizabethan style of presentation. He threw out the trappings and the gorgeous scenery, which demanded the rearranging and revision of the script, and returned to 'pure' Shakespeare.

He made a number of interesting moves. During a time of opulence in staging, he insisted on a bare stage. And not only that; he made every effort to have his plays performed in the open air. As anyone who has done this knows, the audience is often running for cover in a downpour. This was the result for Greet on many occasions, according to the reviews I read.

The fact that he presented Shakespeare in the open air was an interesting innovation in itself. He was suggesting, in fact, that the people 'come to the play' rather than 'go to the theatre'. An extra little wrinkle of interest is that they were normally played on a university campus, a location in Canada at that time not usually associated with theatre. Today, of course, the university circuit is quite popular. Here, in the land of the gown, we have dollars to disperse and a captive audience built into a plush multi-media environment. But in Greet's time it wasn't so attractive. To determine on this course, then, he needed an underlying purpose that was obviously not geared to the entertainment business. It seems to me that Greet's main concern was to educate. Although I have no evidence, I wouldn't mind making a small bet that Ben and some of his actors expected to make an appearance in the odd seminar between performances.

According to the *Toronto Globe,* 13 May 1905, Greet made a regular habit of performing in the residence garden at the University of Toronto. (This was, by the way, noted as being his third season). In this year he was presenting *The Tempest* and *The Two Gentlemen of Verona.* I found the *Globe's* method of handling theatre criticism quite interesting and at first confusing. Apparently they used two critics on a regular basis—two critics who obviously had very little to do with one another. One would write a preview of what was coming up, usually saying eagerly that he looked forward to the performance to see whether it confirmed his opinions. The other would write the review after the performance. Until you recognize this—that there were two not one—you get a strange feeling that you are being 'put on'. The contradictions and snide remarks only make sense when you recognize two critics at work.

The first review I found looked forward to Greet's arrival, and especially to see how Greet would avoid the 'Spectacular of the Storm and the wreck at Sea', in *The Tempest.* He raised my curiosity, I must confess. He assumed that they would get around it by the 'heroic process of excision'. Noting that this was habit now and that *The Tempest* and *A Midsummer Night's Dream* usually suffered 'much mutilation and adaptation', he concluded his article by commenting that there was *no* record of *The Tempest* ever having been performed in Toronto.

I eagerly turned forward to find the review. (Remember, of course, that I expected the same man to be writing.) I found not a word on staging—the difficulties of the wreck at sea seemed furthest from his mind! Rather, the critic turned his adroit mind to questions of whether or not *The Tempest* was really a very good play.

146

It was, in his opinion 'not one of the best of the author's acting dramas.' Before ending his review he reminded his readers—and obviously the other critic—that *The Tempest* 'has not been seen produced in Toronto within the memory of the *younger* generation'!

Both reviews are poor specimens for the researcher. They are chatty and inconsequential. They spend little time on what is happening, concentrating on what has happened in the past or what might have happened. Presumably, they felt that they were educating the public. To me, they appeared as another example of what someone recently has called 'communication pollution'. It is not valuable! At the risk of being struck down by lightning or a thunder bolt from the god that protects Stratford, I would venture to say that much of what Nathan Cohen says today in the *Star* will be valuable to theatre historians in the future! Because he usually says something pertinent to the production!

Here is a part of a review of *A Midsummer Night's Dream* performed by Greet in 1909, again in Toronto:

> Probably no play by Shakespeare has suffered so great a degree of mutilation, alteration or interpolation at various times as *A Midsummer Night's Dream*. It has been treated as the libretto of an Opera, transformed into a masque, and converted into a gorgeous spectacle in which the scenery, dresses and lighting become the chief considerations. One may come to the conclusion from reading the chronicles of the English stage that managers depended upon the grotesque comedy of Bottom and his companions or upon interpolated music, masques and business to make the piece go with the public.

This sort of critical writing is frustrating to a researcher because it has literally nothing to say about the particular event. Maybe if more critics tucked in the back of their minds that they were writing for future generations of researchers they would serve their own public better!

As usual, the American critics of the past have presented more information about actual productions than the Canadians have for their country. It is difficult to guess why this is the case. It is possible that the American people and critics were just more interested in this aspect of the Drama. Canadians have obviously tended to be more literary–minded and serious about the whole business. If only theatre could just be drama and we could keep our hands clean! When Greet performed *Julius Caesar,* for example, the critic had this to say:

147

Julius Caesar is but rarely put on the stage and its production locally yesterday proved more instructive and interesting to students of the great poet. The reciting of the play was followed throughout with most respectful and absorbed attention.

Poor Shakespeare! Indeed, it is the living Shakespeare, the craftsman of the stage who suffered in Canada. The stage was not active in the sense that it was in the United States. As I have said, we had opera houses, but they were used mainly by touring companies from England and the United States. This fact in itself became a dead weight. Canadians very early in the game became receivers of culture. Unfortunately, as receivers we had little protection—or I might say, finding ourselves in that position, we didn't care enough to screen the shows (as we do not today, in fact, with much of our television) and as a result we picked up a massive amount of junk.

This, naturally enough, tended to turn the educated people against the theatre in general. Many of our would-be playwrights actually turned their backs on the stage and wrote poetic dramas. Before taking a closer look at this type of drama in Canada, we should probably take a minute to try to define it and explain its beginnings as a movement in England.

Generally this movement took place in England at approximately the time experiments in realistic drama were being made. It was considered a worthy endeavour, perhaps inevitable, in revulsion against the popular farce, pantomime, acrobatic display and extravaganza to be found rampant on the stage. The experiment, however, was not an unqualified success. As William Archer noted when reviewing the poetic drama:

> The indubitable fact remains, that while effort in the direction of poetical drama has been frequent and strenuous, success has been, to say the least of it, exceedingly rare.

Because it did not prosper, the movement received little critical attention.

What was this literary and poetic theatre? Generally speaking it was known as 'poetic drama', a term that became a familiar expression in the early part of the nineteenth century. However, its beginnings have not been studied to any extent and as far as I know no full account of its development has yet been written. Originally it was generally a copy of Elizabethan drama, but in the latter part of the nineteenth century it underwent a change

148

which altered its form. According to Priscilla Thouless, 'The coming of naturalistic drama killed the old ideal of the poetic dramatists—the romantic drama, written in a tradition alien to modern times', and forced some of the writers 'to create new poetic forms of drama.'[4] Ernest Reynolds also draws attention to the division when he notes that 'it was not until Shaw's preaching of Ibsenism in the 'nineties had begun to take effect that there was any appreciable stirring of English poetic drama towards a new synthesis of social expression.'[5] There are clearly then, two kinds of poetic drama: the old, which was basically a copy of Elizabethan drama, and the new, which attempted to capture the modern temper and was written by such diverse poetic dramatists as William Butler Yeats, John Drinkwater and George Bottomley.

In examining the poetic dramas of the Canadian writers we will find ourselves totally concerned with the pseudo-Elizabethan variety. These were the plays of the old ideal, written by poets who, as someone has said, 'were plot dramatists, dressing up their stories in Shakespearian peacock feathers.'

I won't bore you with the long list of these so-called playwrights, but maybe I could select one or two just to give you a glimpse of their style.

Our most famous one I suppose is Charles Heavysege—Shakespeare and the Bible were his models. *Saul* was his most important play of which one critic of the time was able to say that some of the better passages were 'scarcely short of Shakespearean.' Here is an excerpt:

> Now let me die, for indeed I was slain
> With my three sons. Where are ye sons?
> Oh let me find ye, that I may perish with thee: dying,
> Cover you with my form, as doth the fowl her chickens.

That is not 'short of Shakespearean'. I cheated a bit in selecting but swear to you that nowhere in the play does Heavysege approach Shakespeare. He merely executes the one-step by imitating Shakespeare.

John Hunter-Duvar is another Canadian poetic dramatist of our past. He wrote a play called *The Enamorado*. Here is a familiar-sounding description of the dawn:

> See the gates
> Are swinging on the hinges of the east,

---

4   Priscilla Thouless, *Modern Poetic Drama*, (Oxford, 1934) p. 8.
5   Ernest Reynolds, *Modern English Drama*, (Norman, 1951) p. 73.

And out there wells the flush of morning red
That heralding the coming of the sun
Encarnadines our lovely ladies' cheeks
Making them living roses.

Shakespeare in Canada sometimes helped solidify those very characteristics in Canadians that assured the atrophy of the theatre. Through him they hoped to make a respectable escape from the theatre 'trash' of the times. In the name of Shakespeare they sometimes denied the theatre. They wrote closet plays in the Shakespearian manner thereby divorcing themselves from the rough-and-tumble of the stage. Their motives may be defended but the end result was fatal. Their determination to raise the level of drama to a higher plateau was praiseworthy but by turning their backs on the actors and directors they produced only dead drama.

As I suggested earlier, Shakespeare can be considered a barometer. Following the reaction to him we can search a little deeper into the psyche of the culture in which he is placed. He apparently polarized in many instances the moral, social and political drives in the United States, whereas in Canada he revealed the separation between these drives.

But that was the past. Today we still have our dear old barometer and if we look carefully at Shakespearian productions today, I think we may find some indications of a change in the cultural weather in this northern part of the New World.

THE STILL AND THE SMILE

W. B. Ready

Exegesis is autopsy, the probing within the living body to discover the soul of it, and it is doomed to failure from the start. Consider Tolkien's attack on exegesis in his lecture to the British Association in 1936, *Beowulf and the Critics*. It is a rousing attack upon the exegetes who will take a work apart to seek the reason—reason! —of its creation, and then examine each piece separately, reducing the whole thing to rubble, failing thereby ever to see what the work was to begin with. Shakespeare is done to death daily by disciples of literary exegesis. Exegesis is a great mouthful of a word. It sounds like a disease, and so it is; and exegetes are the carriers of it. Exegesis is the killer of the Dream; it pours into words what is beyond their power to contain. Exegetes fail when they try to relate in words the spirit of man, the joy that can come to him, out of the blue. Dream is our armour against Truth. We are such stuff as dreams are made of, if perchance—there's the rub, perchance —we are allowed to dream.

It is beyond the power of words to express meaning that is common to us all. Words are allusive, are as much a part of our psyche as the very Ego. Words spell us down; we are tongue-tied without them, and yet because they allow us some communication, and that only within groups, we cling to the illusion— we are great clingers to illusions, like drowning mariners to a spar —that through words we are capable of understanding and transmitting our understanding of that soul within us. This soul we do not understand, and can only recognize when we are surprised by joy or sorrow, the soul within us that lies far beyond the power or even the comprehension of words. Words such as these are all very well, but even with *hwyl* they are a most rudimentary form of communication. Something lies beyond the word, something dark and tenuous and full of hope, like the shadow that lies between the arm of Adam and his side, as God touches his finger, in Michelangelo's painting of our beginning on the ceiling of the Sistine Chapel of the Vatican.

In the beginning was the Word, 'In Principio erat Verbum,' John the Gospel-maker wrote, a fine poetic phrase, but that is just what the Word is—the beginning, no more. In these days of Mars, and the moon landing, we all seem to take it for granted that the life that we will discover there will be like our own, or there will be no life there at all. They will discover life, be assured of that, they already have. A germ of this earth has lived there for three years and returned to earth, so far relating, however, only to his brother germs. For us to think that Moon life will even remotely resemble the life that we know, is so presumptuous and so innocent that it makes us want to coddle and dandle the whole world of our learning, for within us we are all asking that fine, rhetorical question of the Paycock: 'What is the stars, what is the moon?' Aboard his Flying Dutchman of a ship, lashed to the wheel by a marlinspike, Captain Boyle used to lift his eyes and ask of himself that question, that Joxer Daly would agree, was a darling one. And so it is, a darling question. And the captain did not wait for an answer. We are naive, worth saving, as long as we believe in this life beyond us, there will be those who know of daffodils that come before the swallows dare, and take the winds of March with beauty, who know of violets dim that are sweeter than the lids of Juno's eyes; know the pale primroses that die unmarried before they behold Phoebus in his strength; the bold oxlips and the crown imperial, lilies of all kinds . . . This cannot be, but there is hope for us as long as we believe it. The Word, then, is the beginning and we are all encased in it. And yet in those few lines of Shakespeare we fly free of it, to Elysium. The warehouse of our words, our thesaurus, does not contain enough store to bring us to the end we seek, that end we do not know, nor even clearly realize that we seek it; it is all love in a mist. Words need transmutation. The Philosophers know that and are all tangled up in it, that is what alchemy is all about.

All that is the soul of man, and 'soul' I use for lack of a better word, is led astray by words. We think of words as a common currency, whereas they are allusive and as different and as alike as twins or sisters. It has been the great treason of the scholars, the great *trahison des clercs,* that they have reduced to words the sacred flame and filtered the kill through wordy ashes, to daub those beyond the pale of their *wissenschaft,* so that the young and ardent of every generation wipe it off, and the others swallow it like a physic, accept the culture, place big books on their coffee tables and subscribe to *Life, Time* and even the *Saturday Review* in its name.

152

Christ, most of all, has suffered from treason. We clerks still have men accepting, few denying, their story of bodies bursting from the graves on Judgement Day; have reduced the dream of the Rood, the Crucifixion, to a plastic image on a dashboard of a car. They have replaced the sonorous magnificence that goes beyond the words of *Dies Irae, Stabat Mater, Tantum Ergo* with hootenanny jingles, campfire songs, freedom claps. The guitar has become the liturgical instrument.

It is neither blasphemous nor profane to couple Shakespeare with Christ, for he, most of all men, is part of that creative process which in its amalgam is the godhead. I speak oddly, perhaps, as a souper, a maverick in the club of clerisy, in denying the final virtue to the Book, to the printed word. The Book is a depository, that is all, containing clumsily, yet better than any other method, that is all, the canon of the genius of man. But it is humbug about the Book being the life-blood of a master spirit. The Book is anything but a placebo. It is no cure-all for all that pricks and goads the troubled, restless youth, nor is it ever solace that will replace action, and most books are downright bad and banal.

The genius of Shakespeare is like a djin. It is beyond words but will rise out of them and show a glorified body when in the strangest places and to the oddest people, like Alf's Button, if only the people get their hands on it and come to it with the proper disposition which may be far from the classroom as we know it, and are allowed full access to it without library regulations or the block who would break it down into syllables and syntax structures.

Anthony Burgess has remarked that the bust supposed to be of the Bard that reposes in Stratford is not that at all, but a costive likeness of a commercial traveller who was wont to spend his dreary nights away from home in the sort of hotels where these poor wretches totted up their daily score of calls. Yet Matthew Arnold, contemplating such a bust, wrote of Shakespeare that he was a man surpassing knowledge, of whom you will forever ask and ask, and in return will never get more than his still smile. Now the still of my title is not that sort of still at all, nor like the still of the silence that was at Appomattox; the stillness that surrounds a great event. I speak of a still that stews and brews; distills, loosens the tongue, kindles the eye, and lets the rest of the world go by. C. E. Montague had some appreciation of the sacredness of this kind of still in his story, *Another Temple Gone,* where there is at the beginning a heart of silence. There is still in the eye of every great event, and around it everything goes whirling on. This area of silence has its deep, deep ease, as still as the core of the axle that holds the wheel. All about it the wheel is turning any way it likes, or thinks it is turning any way it likes. But a lovely stillness comes from the heart of the still which holds the essence of it all. If in our life, if we can but reach that area of silence, now and then, we are become blessed. Peaceful with that still was the town of Gartumna, in the troubled days of unrest during a land war in Ireland; so peaceful and quiet it was, that the Establishment needs to be, when within its structure there arises a carefree and unconcerned union, an area that is not concerned with its busy going-on.

Anyone who needs the beat of a different drum and walks out of step, has flowers in his hair, in his hand, or in his mind, and talks to himself, is suspect and daft—according to the ways of the world. So the Establishment raided the town of Gartumna with their constables, and found there a still. Before they arrested the keeper of that still and dismantled it, the still, that was the heart of the peace there, the police took a draft of the creation, a draft, a thoughtful and absorbed tot. The sergeant of the raiding police did not cross himself, or take off his boots as if he was on holy ground, since he was neither a Catholic nor a Mussulman, but he felt his soul draw off from this clamorous and bustling world into a cloistered and a calm retreat. One of his constables had begun to toss the potion down his throat, but his gullet reacted at this ignorant swilling. He began imbibing it, drop by drop, like the sacramental wine it was in essence and he realized, as he sipped it slowly, what a fool he had been to gulp it, to be a policeman. To swill this potion was to use the great Garrick as a spear carrier, a super. The potable sum of all the embodiments of majesty, love, comedy and tragedy were in the still at Gartumna. The still of it entered the frames, the big-boned, red-necked frames of these Constabulary.

The still of Shakespeare seeps through his learning, through his teaching, and through his life. Somehow, this great master of languages broke through the crust of the alphabet, through the spelling into still, into the supernatural. It is a spelling at first and the conjure is reading simple and easy. We can get through words, through their action into an area where heaven lies.

Some people possess a visual imagination, others a verbal. Sometimes, the imagination is purely visual, sometimes purely verbal, often mixed. Think, for instance, of the number five. Some of you will see a five, others will hear the word five; and others of you, believe me, will hear five ding-dongs, and this is only the beginning. What five means to all of us, is not at all what it means to each one of us. Five is a word that might cause some pulses to quicken, eyes to light, tears to fall, who knows? The word, the print itself, are not enough to convey the meaning that lies beyond them. I have contended for years that one does not have to read a book to learn it, if the book is great enough. Who, for instance, has read *Don Quixote?* Damn few; and most of them admit that to read *Don Quixote* in the original is beyond the capacity of most men. To understand all of the allusions within the text would baffle even a scholar of *Hispanidad* yet somehow, the idea of Don Quixote, the spirit of the book, has come through to us clearly and has been accepted among us as admirable and well-nigh divine; even in the musical *Man of La Mancha*, some of this shows through. This foolish knight, surrounded by the grinning real fools in the world, like us, somehow gains the affection of mankind far more than does, for instance Cyrano de Bergerac. Quixote is a great man of the west, and it is something which seems to me to be peculiar to western man, that this idea of Don Quixote has captured the whole imagination of the west, from long before the great idea of sacrifice as portrayed by Christ.

It is to be found in the Gaelic legends, in the story of Cuchulain, the Hound of Ulster. It is to be seen most of all, I think, in the legends of the Norse, in which sacrifice and suffering are nearly all, all that's worth living for, with no reward as promised at the end and no surrender possible, save death.

To live in hope, the hope of some pie in the sky, where we'll wander around with wings, blowing horns, plucking harps, and eating custard, is inexpressibly vulgar to this ideal. Perhaps the greatest contribution that America has given to the world is in her imaginative use of this great attribute of western man. The cowboy movie, I think, is America's greatest contribution to culture. Here we see, pure and undefiled, a man riding in from nowhere, into a frame town where he rights wrong, maybe is killed in doing so, and all for no reward, no reward on this earth. If he survives he rides on to another town, on to a dusty death, or his own corruption someplace else. I have never seen this idea denied, even in desert camps.

Shakespeare, and there must be a sigh of relief among many of you that at last I have come to him, is the greatest man who has ever lived. He has conjured up for us a world beyond that where we walk and spend our time; the world that is still much with us, a world where getting and spending we lay waste our powers. Of this world, Shakespeare is the one-man wonder, England's pride, the envy of the world, and for all his Cleopatras and Othellos, and kilted Scots, and Jewish gabardine he was, and is, above all, English. English to the bone, to the very marrow of that bone. During his own time he was regarded but as a member of that goodly company of poets and dramatists. England, at that time indeed, was a nest of singing birds, and among those birds there was in William Shakespeare a whole exaltation of larks, and the rest were mere swallows, even sparrows, as compared to him. In terms of venery, the other writers of his age were but a murder of crows, a laughter of turkeys, a gaggle of geese, a tiding of magpies. He was, himself alone, exaltation itself. The praises of his crowd were nothing much, but this should be no surprise. Naked hatred, dislike, envy and malice peer out of the eyes of any man, when introduced to a fellow writer. I have never yet heard, nor do I expect to, nor would it be right if I did, genuine praise come from one writer about a rival; any more than I expect to hear words of praise about university administrators from faculty men.

Shakespeare, in his time, looked like a mundane man, a plump, well-to-do playwright, a man of business with a shrewd and dubious eye, an eye always upon the audience, on the gate, or the powers that be. There was nothing in his background, nothing in his education, nothing in his milieu that could have led him to greatness; greatness that surpasses all other greatness that has been given to man. He was given to us by the theatre; it was the theatre that made him, not him the theatre. The theatre was his chosen implement, but the implement was there ready to his hand; he did not innovate, he did nothing new; there were plays similar to his before, and there were to be plays based upon the same structure as his later. Indeed, he took the clay of the common substance of the drama and fashioned out of it the wondrous being that has brought joy to the world.

Never forget that despite the ugly text books, despite the syntactical teaching, the verbal memorizing, the dreadful annotations, all the exegesis, Shakespeare is beloved still by the young. The schools have not murdered him. A place like Stratford has saved him from the power of the Dog. This is the benefit of seminars on the Man, where we are divorced for a while from the print of him and shown the living theatre of the great one.

He still calls the people and still they come. I do not mean the students or the learned few, but all the people.

The general reader has ceased to be. Consider for a moment England's greatness—her only true greatness—her literature, and compare it with literature of any other land in the world, especially in the world of English. Recently, the *Times Literary Supplement* devoted an issue of 176 pages to the English Literary Imagination, its strength and its scope. In every field they yielded the palm of these days to the writers of North America, the other real world of English. This was hard for them: giving up their all. But for the centuries that followed Shakespeare, the motherland of the English tongue was, like the race horse, Eclipse: First, and the rest were nowhere. Consider the start line to be 1500, and give the French, for instance—who else matters? Japanese? Italian?—a one hundred-years' handicap. Their entries are Rabelais, Ronsard, Du Bellay, Montaigne, Molière, Pascal, Racine and Madame de Sevigne. Then, carrying a century of weight, starting at 1600, the English runners for the Helicon Stakes were Campion, Crashaw, Herbert, Vaughan, Donne, Jonson, Milton, Marvell, Bunyan, the King James versioneers (the whole forty-seven of them) and leading them by laps, Shakespeare. The French were mere plugs, not in the same race, on the same course.

Yet Shakespeare alone, of them all, calls to the people now. Maybe some still read Rose Macaulay's novel of Herrick, *They Were Defeated*. There is Milton scholarship abounding. We cheat now and then, and reach across the tape maybe to Pope, Defoe and Swift, who all started about the time of the end of my imaginary race, but Shakespeare is the beloved one, the only winner: First, and the rest are nowhere. The specialists, exegetes, have taken over all of them, barring Shakespeare. Shakespeare writes for us still. We are in a time of political assassinations. Julius Caesar is as timely now as ever, Macbeth we saw recently transformed into MacBird. A West Side story of Romeo and Juliet was a pop hit on stage and film. There is a Greek girl on the island of Cyprus even today whispering to her lover-boy from the Turkish side: 'How cam'st thou hither, tell me, and where fore?/The orchard walls are high and hard to climb/And the place death considering who thou art,/If any of my kinsmen find thee here.'

Somewhere in the world of English every night is Shakespeare. There are living shrines to his name in New England, in the place of his birth, in London . . . The best producers seem to find in him the challenge that wakes their talents (the recent productions of *Henry V*, for example), Olivier's great new Shylock, the television and radio adaptors (the great scenes of the historical plays recently presented by the BBC). There is an audience, a congregation for him in every school production. The common speech of the English is strewn with Shakespeare. There are those who read or hear him always on their way to work, and when they encounter love, ingratitude, familiar situations, the insolence of power, it is his words that form in their minds, often without their being aware of the fount.

I was a soldier once, unmartial though I be, but for nearly six years I did service. It has been the most important time of my life up to now, and among the soldiers of Shakespeare I feel at ease today. When the tunes of glory are muted, brayed or rendered dissonant, I still can walk freely among the camp with Hal, cower under the rock with Falstaff, and listen to the old Celtic brag.

I get joy like the morning when I recall those words of Hotspur and Sir Richard Vernon at the rebel camp near Shrewsbury. Hotspur is looking for a bloody fight and for honour—he hears the king is come in arms against him:

HOTSPUR: He shall be welcome too. Where is his son,
            The nimble-footed madcap Prince of Wales,
            And his comrades, that daffed the world aside
            And bid it pass?

VERNON: All furnished, all in arms;
            All plumed like estridges that with the wind
            Bated like eagles having lately bathed;
            Glittering in golden coats, like images;
            As full of spirit as the month of May,
            And gorgeous as the sun at Midsummer;
            Wanton as youthful goats, wild as young bulls.
            I saw young Harry, with his beaver on,
            His cuisses on his thighs, gallantly armed,
            Rise from the ground like feathered Mercury,
            And vaulted with such ease into his seat
            As if an angel dropped down from the clouds
            To turn and wind a fiery Pegasus,
            And witch the world with noble horsemanship.

Hotspur is a great one for honour. remember his encounter with Worcester:

            By heaven, methinks it were an easy leap
            To pluck bright honour from the pale-faced moon,
            Or dive into the bottom of the deep,
            Where fathom-line could never touch the ground,
            And pluck up drowned honour by the locks
            So he that doth redeem her thence might wear
            Without corrival, all her dignities.

Yet Falstaff, Shakespeare's greatest creation—so great is he that it lies yet beyond the power of man to play him, 'yet banish plump

Jack and you banish all the world',—says of honour, as he cowers while battle rages, and the young lions seek for the bubble,

FALSTAFF: Hal, if thou see me down in the battle, and bestride me so, 'tis a point of friendship.

PRINCE: Nothing but a colossus can do thee that friendship. Say thy prayers, and farewell.

FALSTAFF: I would 'twere bedtime, Hal, and all well.

PRINCE: Why, thou owest God a death.   *(Exit)*

FALSTAFF: 'Tis not due yet, I would be loath to pay Him
            before his day.
            What need I be so forward with him that calls not on
            me? Well,
            'tis no matter. Honour pricks me on. Yea, but how if
            honour prick me off when I come on?
            How then? Can honour set to a leg? No. Or an arm?
            No. Or take away the grief of a wound? No.
            Honour hath no skill in surgery, then? No. What is
            honour? A word. What is in that word, honour?
            What is that honour? Air. A trim reckoning!
            Who hath it? He that died o' Wednesday.
            Doth he feel it? No. Doth he hear it? No.
            'Tis insensible, then? Yea, to the dead. But will it not
            live with the living? No. Why? Detraction will not
            suffer it. Therefore I'll none of it. Honour is a mere
            scutcheon.

This is that old lad of the castle who said: 'I have more flesh than other men, and therefore more fraility.'

Falstaff, a genial, sinful man like us who knows how easy it is to make a man laugh with a tale of skullduggery, if that man has never had an ache in his back, sees his good fortune smash against the icy majesty of the king who used to be the wanton boy.

In the joking scene in *Henry IV, Part I*, where Falstaff and Hal did a barroom turn of guying Hal's father, the king, Falstaff makes the great plea for the good times to continue past their allotted time and beseeches the king not to banish him from the sun of the world that revolves around the crown, but the young prince says, and means it: 'I do, and I will.' Just after that, a knocking sound is heard off-stage. It is the knocking of the gate that tells that the end of good times is coming in. Then there is the smile that is in every Englishman when he thinks about the Welsh. Glendower boasts of his Celtic arcane powers, of the earth shaking at his birth, of the heavens flaming, and what do you think of that, Englishman? And English Hotspur says: 'I think no man speaks better Welsh.' 'I can call spirits from the vasty deep,' Glendower persists. 'Why so can I, or so can any man,/But will they come when you do call for them?' Glendower, Welsh as ever, goes on, 'Why, I can teach you, Cousin, to command the Devil.' And Hotspur: 'And I can teach thee, Coz, to shame the Devil,/By telling Truth; tell Truth, and shame the Devil.' Hotspur's apologies for his cavalier treatment of Harry's envoy who demanded for his king the custody of prisoners reflects the grim, dour humour of the infantry.

HOTSPUR: My liege, I did deny no prisoners.
But I remember, when the fight was done,
When I was dry with rage and extreme toil,
Breathless and faint, leaning upon my sword,
Came there a certain lord, neat, and trimly dressed,
Fresh as a bridegroom, and his chin new reaped
Showed like a stubble-land at harvest-home.
He was perfumed like a milliner,
And 'twixt his finger and his thumb he held
A pouncet-box, which ever and anon
He gave his nose and took it away again;
Who therewith angry, when it next came there,
Took it in snuff; and still he smiled and talked,
And as the soldiers bore dead bodies by,
He called them untaught knaves, unmannerly,
To bring a slovenly unhandsome corse
Betwixt the wind and his nobility.
With many holiday and lady terms
He questioned me, amongst the rest, demanded
My prisoners in your Majesty's behalf.
I then, all smarting with my wounds being cold,
To be so pestered with a popinjay,
Out of my grief and my impatience,
Answered neglectingly I know not what,
He should, or he should not; for he made me mad
To see him shine so brisk, and smell so sweet,
And talk so like a waiting gentlewoman
Of guns and drums and wounds—God save the mark!—
And telling me the sovereign'st thing on earth
Was parmaceti for an inward bruise;

And that it was great pity, so it was,
This villainous salt-petre should be digged
Out of the bowels of the harmless earth,
Which many a good tall fellow had destroyed
So cowardly; and but for these vile guns,
He would himself have been a soldier.

Shakespeare has to be saved from the evil of exegesis, drunk at the still, be learned with a smile, although like a blinding flash some learned lover, some master of the language art, some exegete, may reveal to us something further of the great rubric or canon. Most of those who wear the gown, the chasuble of the Shakespearian priesthood, are about as worthy a lot as followed the Carmelite; the Arabic pattern of dance and song before the altar, making of this glorious ritual a daily joy. Shakespeare is something to be taken, then, as a spiritual drink and all the thespians who have trod the boards spouting the wonder that he can rouse within us and surprising us by joy, are a part of the price we pay for making of the man a part of our imagination.

The greatest fortune that ever came to Will was that he was born to England; and English was his tongue; would that it were mine, and I were English. I lack the ability to read Li Po, Cervantes, Goethe, Comenius in their original tongue, yet I am convinced out of ignorance, from which comes probably all true faith, that English is the loveliest language of the world, and at the time of Shakespeare, the writers were more than a mere nest of songbirds, they were an exaltation of larks, as they were in their garments a bouquet of pheasants; a very dazzle of zebra.

So let us rejoice this time that has brought us together, let us drink our fill at the still, the smile will follow as the night follows the day.

KING ALFRED'S COLLEGE

LIBRARY

THE WOMEN'S COLLEGE
LIBRARY